Flirting for Women

The Ultimate Guide on How to Flirt Like Cleopatra and Use Non-Verbal Communication and Seduction Techniques to Start Dating High-Value Men

Contents

Introduction

Everyone flirts, but some people are better at it than others. Flirting has a lot of benefits if you do it correctly. For instance, a person can get out of difficult situations by flirting his or her way out. Women are experts at flirting, but due to the rapidly changing world, many women have lost their edge in the world of flirting; that does not mean that these edges cannot be *sharpened!* This guide is sure to help women who want to practice and hone their flirting skills.

This book is a great guide for everyone. Even if you are new to the world of flirting, you will learn a lot from this book. It does not matter whether you have flirted before or not; this book will help everyone who wants to learn to flirt.

There are many different books related to flirting and seduction available on the market; they are quite popular as well. The one in your hands stands out from all the other books because, along with experts, many experienced and "qualified" flirters have collaborated in the book, making it highly readable and simple to understand. It is up-to-date and has a lot of new tricks, techniques, and strategies that you can use to flirt with your date; this book can work wonders for a woman who needs a little help with flirting.

Chapter One: Understanding Men and How They Really Think

Men – and many women - believe that women are complex and complicated creatures who are difficult, if not impossible, to understand. Still, many people realize that men are complex too. Decoding their minds and psyches is necessary for understanding them.

Due to the unfortunate stereotypes perpetuated about gender, men and women often have misunderstandings, believing some untrue myths about each other. Demystifying these myths can help both men and women to understand the dynamics of the society in a better way. In this section, let's look at how men think about women. This chapter specifically focuses on some of the most common misguided notions that men have about women, providing useful information about how to reassure men while flirting.

Fortune

Many men think that women love money, luxury, and that they are obsessed with material possessions. Everyone loves material pleasure, but only a few are "hooked" on it. It is not a common fixation. In fact, many women tend to avoid men whose main fixation in life is money and material wealth. Women care for men's passion, work ethics, hobbies, and ambition, more than how rich they are. This approach is seen in other factors too. If a man or woman is interested in only talking about money, then it is better to avoid dating them at all.

Physique

Another common myth that men associate with women is that they are obsessed with men with perfect and highly chiseled bodies. Most women find extremely buff guys off-putting or intimidating. They find these men judgmental and vain as well. No one likes to be self-conscious, and men in great physical shape can make women self-conscious. Similarly, no woman will appreciate it if her man spends more time at the gym instead of spending time with her. Caring about one's appearance is important - but not for the sake of others.

Size of Your Manhood

This is one of the most rampant myths that men associate with women. Most women do not care about the size of your penis, so the concept that "bigger is better" is just a myth. Penile size has become a benchmark for the masculine ego, but almost all penis sizes are acceptable (and enjoyable) for women. Your penis size says nothing about you or your personality, and certainly does not confirm your sexual potency and prowess. The only thing it does confirm is that you have a *big appendage between your legs!* Many men tend to develop self-confidence issues due to their penis size – a dastardly side effect of pornography and "big phallocentric" media culture. Women are more concerned about your personality and your attitude in bed - as well as outside of the bed. They care if you are an attentive and giving lover. They would prefer you to be with a man with a small penis - but a lot of techniques and passion - rather than dealing with a man with a giant penis, but zero understanding of pleasure.

Vulnerability

Vulnerability is another aspect that men think that women think is disgusting and unsexy. Many men even believe it to be unmanly as well. Showing appropriate emotions and feelings at appropriate times and situations is crucial for emotional health, physical health, and mental stability. Women love men who are in touch with their emotional side, men who can express their feelings without being uncomfortable. Men believe that women will judge them if they display their feelings in an obvious manner, but women find it sexy when men can display their emotions.

Women love men who are emotionally stable. This means that women love men who can cry while watching a sad movie and can display their emotions in appropriate situations. This does not mean that the man should go around moping and crying all the time, but true vulnerability shows ingenuity.

Putting Them on a Pedestal

Nobody in this world is perfect, and nobody likes to be treated like a god or goddess all the time. People like to enjoy the simple pleasures of life, which often come from hardships. Everyone has flaws, and these flaws need to be addressed, but many men believe that women love to be perfect, which is why they tend to put women on a pedestal and shower them with compliments day and night. A few compliments in the right situations and on the right occasions are good, but bombarding women with compliments makes men seem insincere. It often leads to disconnection and disconcertion in the relationship. Women do not like to be worshipped.

Women prefer having a connection with their men. Women love to be treated as equals. No one likes to be treated as superior or as inferior in any relationship; so, keeping up the idealized version and its façade can be quite difficult in the long term. This often leads to the formation of cracks in a relationship, and ultimately, the relationship falters.

Superficiality

Men believe that complimenting women about their looks all the time is the best way to flirt with them. This is obviously untrue. Women like being complimented about their looks, but if a man can think only about one thing worth complimenting them about, then the whole relationship becomes old and clichéd very soon. In fact, it also becomes demeaning, because it shows that your man does not understand that you are much more than your looks.

Men understand that there are many things worth complimenting and noticing about their women, but they are afraid to bring them up because they believe that women will not appreciate it. Women can help their men in such cases by reassuring them and projecting their relationship from an optimistic point of view.

Vanity

Men and women alike believe that women are vainer than men, but this is a myth. Men have been vain since ancient times! Men care a lot about their appearances, especially their hairline, their graying hair, etc. Instead of spending a lot of time on improving appearance, men should concentrate on improving their personality, *as this is what women tend to focus on.*

Many women love gray hair because it makes men look more mature and seductive. Often, women do not care about appearances at all if a man can make them laugh. Instead of trying to hide their insecurities, men should embrace them, and just accept that they are part of who they are *as a human.*

Men and Flirting

In the last section, we saw how men tend to have wrong notions about the perceptions women have about them. Men have certain desires and ideas that rarely get fulfilled because they aren't comfortable presenting their ideas. In this section, let us have a look at some of those ideas, which will help you understand the masculine psyche in a better way.

Drinks

Men love it when women offer to buy them drinks. They feel flattered and elated.

Hair

Men love it when women run their fingers through their hair; if combined with a seductive smile, men will love it! This is an intimate and sensual form of flirting. Do not overdo it, though, or it may seem too erotic or sexual.

Clarity

Men generally do not pick up on clues and cues properly. Therefore, many men often fail to acknowledge your presence or flirting, just because they have never been flirted with before. If you feel that the man you are flirting with is not interested in you or that he does not understand what you are doing, then try to be as clear as possible. In most cases, he probably does not know that you are flirting with him. Sometimes, it is better to forgo your coyness and simply flirt.

Smart

Nobody likes fake people, and men are no exception to this rule. Due to some unfortunate stereotypes perpetuated about men, many women think that men do not like women who are confident, bold, and smarter than them. Women think that men feel intimidated by such women. Therefore, many times women try to "dumb down," and while men don't mind bimbos, if you deliberately act like one, then they are sure to see through your game! Plus, it's impossible to continue this fakery for a long time.

Conversation

It is necessary to converse with your date properly. Men like women who can hold a decent conversation on any topic and provides a sign of good chemistry.

Makeup

While you should never apply makeup to please others, you can use the magic of beauty products to enhance your *already beautiful features*. Do not overdo it or underdo it if you are doing it for someone else. This does not mean that you should change your style, appearance, or attire for anyone. Stay true to yourself as much as possible.

Compliments

There is hardly anyone in this world who does not like receiving compliments. Men love them too, and they appreciate them more than anyone else because men hardly ever get compliments. Friends and strangers both avoid giving compliments to men. Men love it when women compliment them for a variety of things.

Subtleness

Women often believe that to appear flirty and "available," they need to act overtly sensual and sexual. This is false. Many men prefer subtlety as well. They would rather have women who flirt in a subtle way more than women who act overtly erotic.

Race/Bigotry

Men, especially men of color, hate it when Caucasian women or women other than those of their own race, fetishize them for the color of their skin. This is a shallow approach toward attraction, as it says nothing about their appearance and their personality. If you really want to compliment them for their skin, instead of talking about the color, consider commenting on smooth and beautiful it is. Exotification is a huge problem that needs to be addressed.

Eyes

Sometimes coquettishness is the way to go. To do this, just look into his eyes for a moment and then look away quickly. Almost all men find this attractive.

Self-Confidence

It pays to be yourself. Do not try to fake a personality just to impress a man. Men hate people who are fake. Instead of faking a personality, just try to develop your own personality. For instance, if you like reading, start reading more, if you like to dance, invest some time into it.

Dance

Another thing that many men love but are afraid to do is dance. Men love to dance, but they rarely do it on their own. If you are at a club, pull your man onto the dance floor and dance with him. This will help you create sweet memories as well.

Sense of Humor

Almost all men consider themselves funny, even if they are not. Humor them sometimes by laughing at their jokes, even if they aren't that funny! Laughing is a great way to appreciate the hard work that men put into being humorous. But do not laugh if you ever feel that the humor is crass or disgusting; bigotry should never be tolerated.

Be Yourself

Every individual is different. Try to maintain your individuality. Understand your true self and present it with confidence. If you are not confident with yourself, you will not be able to flirt confidently.

Smiling

Smiling is one of the easiest methods of flirting, but you need to understand how to do it correctly. Many women think that only smiling and doing nothing else is a simple and effective method of flirting that men understand. This is a myth. Men need much more than a smile to understand your intentions. For men, just smiling does not mean flirting.

Chapter Two: Understanding Flirting

Flirting is one of the most natural, yet one of the most complex, human behavioral concepts. It is a highly individualistic concept, which means that every person flirts in a different and singular way. There are many ways of flirting, which include various verbal, non-verbal, physical, and non-physical methods. But before moving on to these methods, it is necessary to understand the concept of flirting itself. In this chapter, let us put flirting under a microscope and try to understand what it is composed of.

Flirting

Flirting was once upon a time known as coquetry. Some people still use this word to define flirting, but the meaning of coquetry has changed slightly over the years. Flirting is often considered to be a form of sexual communication or behavior. While it is true that flirting is deep-set in sexuality and eroticism, discarding it as just a sexual behavior is a grave injustice to the concept. Flirting has developed into a much more complex and highly social behavior now, often accomplished with the help of written or spoken forms of communication. Flirting is also possible with the help of various non-verbal gestures and body movements. It is generally performed to attract a person.

In almost all the cultures around the world, society disapproves of rampant, explicit, and obvious displays of sexual excitement or advances socially. Similarly, such a display is also looked down upon in private settings if the persons are not romantically inclined towards each other. Indirect suggestions and advances often replace such direct displays. These indirect suggestions are a part of flirting.

Flirting generally involves behaving as well as talking in a certain manner that is suggestive. Your manner should suggest intimacy and boldness, albeit always within the rules of social manners and etiquette. This means a direct display of feelings should be avoided. This direct display should be replaced with irony, metaphors, sensual manner, wordplay, and general playfulness. Double entendre and puns are often used for flirting. Body language and bodily gestures such as open stances, hair flicking, eye contact, proximity, brief touches, and others are used as a form of flirting as well. There are many ways of flirting, as stated above, but generally, it is done in a shy, under-exaggerated, or frivolous style.

Verbal Flirting - Verbal Flirting Generally Includes Challenges

The flirter teases the other party by feigning disinterest, asking random questions, etc. This is done to increase (or add) tension to the situation. It helps the flirter to check the intention of the person and the amount of affection present in the situation. This section also includes things such as displaying poise, knowledge, approval, self-assurance, stylish nature, etc. A commanding attitude is another aspect that comes under this section.

Vocal

While flirting, the flirter changes his or her voice and modulates it. For instance, he or she may change the tone, intonation, volume, or pace of the voice. He or she may change all these together as well.

The concept of flirting and what is accepted as flirting varies according to nation and culture. This is due to the varied positions of social etiquette that change according to culture. These rules guide things such as proximity of people, the duration of eye contact, how much touching is permissible, the appropriateness of words, etc. Still, some behaviors are common throughout most cultures. For instance, smiling and head-tilting is a universal form of flirting.

How People Flirt

As said above, flirting is an essential aspect of social interaction. It is excessively common, yet, still difficult to understand. You may see it (or do it) every day, but understanding it is a different concept altogether. A lot of research has been conducted on flirting by psychologists and sociologists alike. In this section of this chapter, let us have a look at different styles of flirting, such as nonverbal and verbal behaviors.

The Five Styles

As per research, flirting can be divided into five major styles of flirting. These styles differ from person to person. Let us now have a brief look at all these styles.

Physical

The individuals who use this style generally flirt by showing physical behavior and using a lot of gestures. They feel comfortable physically and do so instead of using verbal communication cues. They find it easy to show their attraction with various physical cues. The behavior of such people is often considered to be sexual.

Sincere

People who use this style of flirting generally try to form an emotional connection with the opposite person. They try to form a bond with their romantic partner. This is why people who use this form of flirting generally cultivate intimacy early in the relationship. Such people often desire social support and provide it as well. This kind of flirting is generally romantic in nature. But this does not mean that it can't be sexual as well.

Playful

Individuals who use this style of flirting usually flirt in a lighthearted and playful manner as well. They don't care about how their behavior can be interpreted, but instead look at flirting from a satisfying point of view. They don't mind if their flirting does not end up turning into something serious.

Traditional

People who employ this kind of flirting generally tend to behave well. They like to stay in the boundaries of the stereotypical gender roles. This means that they generally allow men to initiate and women to reciprocate. They strictly follow traditional courtship rules. In this style, women generally take a passive role.

Polite

People who tend to have this kind of flirting style look at courtship from a cautious point of view. People may confuse these flirters for being too aggressive, inappropriate, or even needy.

Verbal and Nonverbal Flirting Behaviors

In this section, let us now have a look at the verbal and non-verbal styles of flirting. There are certain traditional roles that are associated with flirting. Here is a small list of these roles:

• Men generally take an active role in the process of courtship. Both men and women believe that a man should always initiate the courtship process.

• Women tend to take on a passive role in the process of courtship. They are receptive to signs, including verbal and nonverbal cues. They use eye contact a lot.

• Eye contact and signaling with eyes are generally used by women; however, both the genders tend to use these gestures a lot. Flirtatious eye contact is a common flirting technique. This is especially common in the beginning stages of courtship and interaction.

- Women generally smile a lot while talking to a person they like. This is generally observed in the later stages of the courtship and interaction.

In the initial stages of the approach, men tend to use various space-maximizing movements. This includes appearing as big as possible by adjusting and extending arms etc. Men also tend to reduce their closed-body positions. These positions include crossings legs, crossing arms, etc.

In the initial stages of interaction and courtship, both partners tend to pay compliments to each other a lot.

Implementing this Information

Understanding flirting techniques is essential. It can help you on these three fronts:

Improvement

You can improve your flirting style if you understand the intricacies of flirting carefully.

Situation

Understanding the nuances of a situation is essential for flirting. You should be able to adapt and change your style of flirting according to the need or time and situation. Similarly, you should also consider the person and his likes and dislikes as well.

Preselection

Understanding the different styles of flirting can also help you develop a smart process of preselection that will help you understand the process of courtship in a better way. It will help you make correct choices. It will also help you understand whether a person is worth knowing or not.

Improving Your Own Flirting Style

It is possible to make your own flirting style more unique and effective if you understand the intricacies of flirting. It can help you understand your weaknesses and work on them. Similarly, it can also help you understand your strengths and make them even stronger.

For instance, if you now realize that you generally use the physical style of flirting, you can utilize it effectively. For instance, you can select situations that require more physical interactions. These include clubbing, dancing, etc. You should generally avoid situations where physical intimacy is either not required or outright impossible- i.e., online.

If you generally use the polite style of flirting, you will notice that it is difficult for you to get your interest noticed by others. It is your natural attitude to act reserved, but if you ever want to display or convey your interest, you will have to change your flirting style slightly. You need to become somewhat forthcoming.

Tailoring Your Flirting

You can also change your flirting style according to your partner. This means that you can change your flirting style in such a way that it can help you understand your partner better. It also means changing and modifying your flirting style according to the flirting style of your partner.

For instance, if your partner loves a playful style of flirting, but you generally use the physical style of flirting, it is recommended to change the style of flirting and make it more playful. If your partner enjoys a more conservative style of flirting, you can adapt your personal style accordingly and make it more conservative.

Deciding Whom to Approach

Understanding the nuances of flirting styles can also help you to choose your future or potential partners. It can allow you to select partners in a much better way. For instance, you can match your flirting style to that of your partner and see whether your flirting style will complement their flirting style or not. If you feel that his flirting style is too different from yours, you may find the interaction difficult.

While the compatibility of flirting styles can really help you significantly, it does not mean that you and your potential boyfriend need to have the same flirting style. It means that you should instead try to adapt your flirting style and modify it to form a more homogenous interaction.

For instance, if you generally use a playful style of flirting, you will notice that this style does not work well with the conservative or polite style of flirting. But it can work well with the sincere style of the flirting and physical style of flirting as well!

While complimentary flirting style can help you with your interactions, it does not mean that you should focus on these styles only. Do not be apprehensive about approaching someone just because your flirting styles do not complement each other. In many cases, people with the opposite flirting styles have had long and successful relationships.

Reminder

While dealing with different styles of flirting, you should always remember that flirting is a highly individualized concept. The five different styles are present in varying amounts in all individuals. This means that a person can have a mixture of traditional flirting style with playful flirting style as well. Many times, people change their flirting style according to the situation. So instead of judging a person right away, try to analyze their personality carefully. This will help you avoid making rash decisions.

In the next chapter, we'll have a look at one of the most common types of flirting in modern times - Online Flirting.

Chapter Three: To Flirt or Not to Flirt Online

One of the greatest gifts of technology and modern times is the Internet. The Internet has made our lives extremely easy and simple. You can find anything and everything on the Internet now. This includes love, as well. In fact, many people find the Internet to be a much better (and quicker) place to find and meet new people as compared to the traditional methods.

According to many people, one of the biggest benefits of online dating is that you can use a variety of filters to nitpick through potential lovers. You can find people who like the same things or hate the same things quickly. Similarly, the Internet can also help you meet people with whom your paths would never cross in real life. But Internet dating and flirting are not all sweet and rosy. There are many cons of Internet dating as well. For instance, online dating can help you find quick dates, but is it really a great place to find someone special who will stay with you forever?

There still exists a stigma against Internet dating. While people do agree that there is a multitude of benefits associated with online dating, they would still rather prefer meeting someone offline. This is due to the regressive portrayal of Internet dating in the media.

Similarly, the overtly romanticized portrayal of traditional dating to have tarnished the image of online dating.

Internet Dating Tips

In this section, let us have a look at some simple Internet or online dating tips that will help you avoid heartbreak and betrayal.

Do Your Research

Before beginning to use online platforms, it is recommended to conduct thorough research. There are many different dating sites and apps available online that offer users a plethora of choices, algorithms, and options as well. Some sites and apps are generic that come with many filters to help you choose men according to your taste. There are some niche dating apps and sites, as well. These can be related to anything, for instance, religion, pets, education, age group, etc. While many people think that online dating is much easier than regular dating, it is not. The only thing easy about online dating is meeting people. Otherwise, like traditional dating, it is also a concept that is based on the trial and error method.

Fewer Photos, More Details

People have become obsessed with posting pictures of their daily lives online. Many people tend to add as many pictures as possible on their dating profiles. Researchers believe that this is a bad strategy if you are trying to attract serious people. Your dating profile should not contain more than five photos. These photos should be curated carefully. They should be able to represent who you are and what your beliefs are. Try to select images that are positive or show your positive side. Showing your negative sides on dating profiles is much worse than showing it offline.

The photos that you choose to upload online should show your true emotions and feelings. It is necessary to pair your pictures with a simple description of yourself. Instead of going for a generic and commonsensical style of expressing yourself, you should try to include something that will prove that you are a unique individual. It should make your profile stand out among the thousands of profiles. Do not expect to get a lot of matches if your profile is generic.

Your profile should hold enough mystery while giving away crucial insights about you. The more truthful you are, the better the chances of meeting interesting people will be. While your insightful profile does not guarantee long-term compatibility, it does mean that you will be able to go on interesting dates. Similarly, it will also ensure that you are going out with a man who shares your likes and dislikes. It will also help you prepare yourself well.

Watch Out for the Lies and the Liars

One of the biggest problems associated with online dating is that people tend to lie a lot while being online. Deception is a rampant problem that plagues online dating. It is easy to fool someone online. A lot of people generally create their own dating profiles, but nowadays, some people also pay people to create dating profiles for them. These professionals are experts in creating dating profiles, which attract people easily. These profiles tend to create a false image of the person.

Catfishing is not a rare problem anymore, but still, your falling into the trap of catfishing attempts is less likely. But this does not mean that you are safe from deception. Many people tend to tell small lies that they think are harmless just to attract dates. The deception is quite gendered as well. For instance, men generally lie about their height or their salary (and almost always about the size of their penis). Women tend to lie about their age. It's clear that these deceptions are based on the stereotypes that are associated with each gender.

Problems

While it is true that online dating has revolutionized the world of dating forever, it has also created a multitude of problems as well. For instance, problems such as "ghosting" and "orbiting" have given rise to stalker-like behavior. Passive stalking is a curse associated with online dating. While passive stalking was always present, online dating has made it easy and more accessible. Before Instagram and Facebook, people still used to creep up on others, but now thanks to social media, this process has become easier and safer.

There are many problems associated with online dating. But this does not mean that online dating cannot help you in many aspects as well. It still is a great way to meet new people. It is a great way to expand your horizons and dating pool as well. But you need to vigilant and constantly aware of the things that happen online.

In the next section, let us have a look at the different Pros and Cons of Online Dating.

Pros and Cons of Online Dating

Online dating is a complex experience. It involves a lot of things – both good and bad. For instance, there are many people who have met their soulmate online. But there are also many women who only receive two things from online dating apps: disappointment and unsolicited pictures of the man's penis. In this section, let us have a look at some of the common pros and cons of online dating.

Let us first have a look at the pros of online dating.

Singles Everywhere

Unlike real life dating where you need to check whether a man is single or not, in online dating, you can be more assured that a man is single. This means you do need to play a guessing game. Similarly, you do not need to guess a man's sexuality; it should be obvious if he is looking for a female mate!

Number

There are a lot of people looking for love online. This means that you will never face a dearth of singles around you.

Ideas

One of the biggest pros of online dating is that you can check out certain details about the man you plan to go on a date with beforehand. This will help you know which topics to broach and which to avoid.

Comfort

Online dating can be done from anywhere- the looking part, i.e., you do not need to go out to find someone and court them.

Expenses

Going out frequently to find potential dates is an expensive affair. Similarly, if you approach matchmakers to find a date for you, you will face a lot of additional expenses as well. Compared to these options, online dating is cost-effective. There are many apps and websites that offer their services for free. The apps that do not offer their services for free offer them quite cheaply. This makes online dating a highly affordable deal.

People

Online dating expands your dating pool to infinity. You can meet some of the most interesting people and get some offbeat stories, as well. Even if you do not end dating, you can always meet new and interesting friends using these apps.

Mate

You may even find your soulmate online (if you search properly) because you will be able to check out and understand everything about your potential date, discarding the ones that do not match your tastes.

Let's have a look at the cons of online dating.

Creeps

You can never guess whether a person is genuine and "good" until you meet them. Online dating sites are full of creepy men, and you can enter dangerous territory quickly. It is difficult to avoid such bizarre personalities online.

Time

Online dating takes a lot of time. You need to weed out a lot of people by checking out their details one by one. It can cause a lot of eyestrain as well.

Online dating can also be quite overwhelming because of the implications associated with it. It is a troublesome experience to reject people based on superficial characteristics.

Rejection

People get rejected all the time, but these rejections are worse online. *Everyone gets rejected online,* but what makes online rejections worse is the fact that they are often superficial. People can reject you based on the vaguest things, including the color of your eyes.

Choice

According to the paradox of choice, the more options we get, the sadder we become because we get befuddled due to the sheer number of choices. The grass is always greener on the other side. This makes your dating life unstable, and you end up going on first dates almost every other day.

Clueless People

Online dating is quite different from real-life dating, and the tactics and techniques that are used in real life are rarely successful in online dating. For instance, women love mysterious men in real life, but they abhor blank profiles online. Blank profiles, incorrect or unflattering photos, lack of details, etc. are some of the most common reasons why online dating can be a nuisance.

Randos

Online dating expands your horizons of dating and allows you to meet people you would never have met in real life. Unfortunately, it does so for everyone, which means that you often get contacted by random men. It is impossible to avoid such people online. These men often try to harass or gaslight women into dating them. While there are options to block or report such profiles online, it does not work all the time. For instance, if you block a creepy man's profile once, he may create another one - just to harass you.

Falsifications

This is one of the biggest problems associated with online dating. Everything is not what it seems in the world of online dating. A person's profile may look great, his pictures may look dazzling, but when he shows up for the real date, all your expectations may shatter immediately. People often lie about themselves online. They act coy and perfect online, but in real life, their real face - and personality - appears.

No Body Language

One of the biggest problems with online dating is that you cannot use body language and gestures. It becomes impossible to judge and understand people properly if you cannot see how they behave and act around other people. Eyes are windows to the soul. In online dating, you cannot see their eyes. Similarly, a lot of deception can happen in online dating.

Online dating is especially difficult for flirting, as you need to depend on texts and voice to do it. Modern flirting uses a lot of gestures and body language to convey non-verbal messages.

It is, therefore, clear that online dating is a complex topic. While it has its benefits, it has a lot of cons as well. It is especially difficult to flirt online. Therefore, it is up to the discretion of the reader, whether to date online or not.

Chapter Four: Appearance: Does it Really Count?

According to many women, a desirable man needs to be kind, intelligent, understanding, family-oriented, etc. Most of these women also believe that men should have a sense of humor and should look decent. But the question is which one of these is the most attractive of all the other traits. According to various research, it has been proven that many people rank every other trait higher than good looks. But this is not reflected in real life generally. In fact, many people tend to focus on good looks more than anything else. While other traits may come into play later, people generally tend to select their mates by looking at their appearance and outer looks first. Everything else comes later. The initial attraction must happen, and that is based on looks whether we like it or not.

Even in online dating, we stop at profiles where the man in the pictures looks charming and attractive. This proves that we do consider good looks or physical appearance to be attractive. In this chapter, let us have a look at this phenomenon in detail.

Physical Attractiveness is More Important Than We Think

Physical appearance and attractiveness are like the gatekeeper to other aspects of a mate. Physical appearance shows that your potential mate is of age, looks healthy, and can reproduce as well. Therefore, physical appearance automatically dominates our mind while choosing a mate. It is pure evolutionary biology. We tend to pursue a relationship with a person who we find attractive. This attraction can be of any kind, but generally, it starts with physical attraction.

Men - both gay and straight - are more inclined to physical attractiveness than women. They understand how important it is. Still, according to research conducted on online dating sites, it was found that both men and women pay close attention to their physical looks and attractiveness. Both care about their general appearance. With this, attractiveness also forms an important part of all our dating decisions. We consider attractiveness more important than intelligence, personality, and education.

According to researchers, physical attractiveness is important to us because we tend to attach certain positive qualities with it. For instance, we tend to believe that the people who are physically attractive are often happier and more pleasant than the individuals who are not physically attractive. Similarly, it was observed that these kinds of associations are present in almost all cultures. The notions of physical attractiveness may change according to culture, but what this attractiveness stands for remains constant. For instance, once upon a time, extreme paleness was highly attractive in Europe, but now it is all about dark skin. Yet, the notions associated with both these factors, i.e., attractiveness equals happiness (and others), remain the same.

There has been a lot of research to counter the research above. In the next section, let us have a look at this research and its results, giving you the full picture.

Physical Attractiveness is Less Important than We Think

According to research, one of the main reasons why we fail to consider the importance of physical attraction is because we do not want partners who are extremely attractive physically. We are satisfied with partners who are just "regularly" attractive. According to research, moderately attractive as well as attractive partners are better than partners who are not attractive at all. Similarly, if a person is less attractive, then he or she is associated with negative qualities. But positive qualities do not require a lot of attractiveness either. If a person is moderately attractive, he or she is associated with positive qualities. This proves that people can find moderately attractive people acceptable and can accept them as a potential mate as well. This might seem to be complicated and convoluted, but to understand this properly, you just need to have a look at the difference between needs and greed.

The difference between needs and greed can help you understand the paradox of moderate levels of physical attraction effectively. A need is something that you like a lot, but if it is available in high amounts, you tend to care less for it. Greed or luxury are not important when the needs are not met. But once the basic needs are met, luxury or greed becomes highly desirable. According to this theory, everyone looks at moderate attractiveness as a need, while anything more than that is a luxury. When people say that physical attractiveness is not important to them, they are most probably always referring to "greed" or a "luxury" level of attractiveness. This means, when people say that they do not care (or do not desire) physical attractiveness, they are talking about the exceptional levels of attractiveness. Of course, they want a person who is moderately attractive, though.

What Exactly is Moderately Attractive?

The concept of moderately attractive is subjective and changes from individual to individual. Everyone agrees that supermodels are incredibly attractive, but everyone disagrees with the definition of moderately attractive. Most attractive people generally have a narrow range of "attractiveness" while people who are less attractive generally have a larger range of "unattractiveness." This means people who are less attractive will consider a lot of people attractive to moderately attractive.

If you and your partner are on the same levels of physical attractiveness, your relationship will most likely last longer. But this is not the only thing that will make your relationship last. There are multiple things to consider if you want to make your relationship last for a long time. Relationships are built on trust and mutual respect. If these two factors are not present in your relationship, no amount of physical attractiveness can salvage it.

Therefore, while physical attractiveness is important, it is not the most important thing in the world. Even if you are not attractive, you will always find a beau who will love you and cherish you forever.

Chapter Five: Confidence - Why It Matters and How to Boost It

No one is born with confidence. It is an acquired trait that people learn over time. No one is fully confident all the time. The levels of confidence fluctuate according to the situation, place, person, and time. Just talking about it will never help you get it. Self-confidence is an essential trait that everyone needs to have. But it is also quite challenging to acquire because of societal pressures. Women find it particularly difficult to develop self-confidence because girls are taught to be shy and coy during their upbringing. Women are taught to be caregivers from birth, which is why we tend to think of others before ourselves. We tend to put the needs of others before our own needs. Therefore, we do not spend a lot of time developing ourselves. Girls are often encouraged to be less daring, to be passive, and less bold. This is done so that we do not become threats to the men around us. But these old practices need to be buried now.

Turn on the television and see how women have changed and how they are becoming more and more self-confident. There are thousands of examples of confident women around you who have changed their world, just based on their self-confidence. These women possess the chutzpah that many other women do not have.

But really, do these women possess something special that others do not? The answer to this question is obviously no. Every woman, or for that matter, every person born in this world has a certain level of chutzpah. This chutzpah remains untouched and is unused. You need to tap into it often to remind yourself of the courage and bravery that you possess.

Self-confidence is essential in every field of life. You cannot do anything successfully if you are not self-confident. Self-confidence is necessary while flirting as well. To flirt with a man requires a lot of strength and confidence. Therefore, many women are afraid of approaching men because they fear facing humiliation and public failure. But this does not mean that you cannot develop self-confidence. Let us now have a look at some tips that can help you become self-confident and bold.

Responsibility

If you want to be self-confident, you need to learn how to take responsibility for yourself. You cannot be self-confident unless you are responsible for yourself. If you wait for things to happen on their own or if you think that Lady Luck will shower her fortunes on you, then you will never succeed in life. Waiting for the guy to hit on, you will take forever. Sometimes it is better to take risks and take things into your own hands. Self-confidence is not magic. No amount of prayers will help you become self-confident. It is a path full of difficulties that you must tread. This path needs to be trodden alone, as well. So, it is time to take matters into your hands and become responsible for your own destiny.

Experiments

These experiments are not related to science. To become self-confident, you need to start experimenting with your life. For instance, if you feel awkward around people, go out and have dinner alone. Join a dance class. Teach yourself new things, such as learning a musical instrument. Test your abilities. Talk to people. See that your abilities are opening new horizons to you.

Action Plan

Every great thing has started with a plan. You cannot achieve success if you do not plan for it. It is recommended to choose a topic and work on it until you develop it thoroughly. These topics can include professional or personal development, as well. It is recommended to develop an action plan and formulate the steps that will take you toward your goal. Making excuses won't cut it. Every tiny step that you take will ultimately take you toward your goal. Every small step will boost your confidence, as well.

Stick to the Plan

Just making the plan is not important; you need to stick to it as well. When you take a new challenge, it is necessary to stick to it as best you can. Self-confidence is not automatic. You need to work hard for it. Each attempt is important, but don't worry if you fail at any point. Just pick yourself up and start working again. Whether you succeed in the long term or not solely depends on how dedicated and passionate you are. Follow through your plan until you taste the sweet taste of success. Do not rest until then.

Act "As If"

Do not wait for the plan to finish to become confident. Confidence is all about faking until you make it. This means that even if you are not confident about something, you just need to work hard and act like you are confident all the time. This is a common psychological trick. You can change your behavior if you believe hard enough. You can change your feelings, your emotions, and your confidence level as well. You just need to believe in yourself and act like you are extremely confident all the time. Once you start faking confidence on the outside, the true, inside confidence will follow soon as well.

Mentor

If you feel that you are not confident and cannot do it on your own, don't worry. You can use the help of a mentor. A mentor is any person related to your field (or not) who is highly dedicated, motivated, and confident. You are supposed to observe them and see how they live their life. For instance, if you are trying to become self-confident about your looks or flirting with men, talk to a woman who is an expert at both things. Observe this woman and learn how she tackles her day-to-day life. Meet the woman and tell her about your problem. Tell her how you plan to solve it. In most cases, this woman will be more than willing to help you. Get her feedback about your action plan. Remember, it is all about faking it until you make it.

Therefore, confidence is something that can be cultivated with ample dedication and practice. It is not difficult to become a person who is confident. You just need to formulate an action plan and work on it meticulously. So do not wait any more, just step up and start working on your confidence right away.

Chapter Six: Play It Like Cleopatra! 3 Ancient Secrets to Attracting Men

Cleopatra is one of the most iconic women in the world. She singlehandedly changed the destiny of the world with the help of her charms, wit, and the power of seduction. Cleopatra is often considered to be one of the top ten queens to ever rule the world.

Cleopatra was the last Pharaoh of Egypt. She was well known for being a legendary seductress. The legends of her seductive powers are still repeated all the time. Every woman can learn from Cleopatra. But before moving on to the things that you can learn from her, it is necessary to have a brief look at her life.

Cleopatra was born in 69 BC. Her father was Ptolemy XII "Auletes," who was a Pharaoh as well. She was the last Pharaoh of Egypt because, during her reign, Rome was ready to take over her kingdom. Cleopatra started her reign side by side with her brother Ptolemy, but this arrangement did not last for too long.

Cleopatra's name has been associated with two men - Mark Antony and Julius Caesar. Both these men were incredibly powerful and strong. She fell in love with Mark Antony after Caesar was brutally murdered by his friends Brutus and Cassius. Many years passed after this, and she finally committed suicide because she lost a battle against a Roman called Octavian.

Her story has been used for various literary endeavors, the most famous being by Shakespeare. After Shakespeare, the person who made her extremely famous was Elizabeth Taylor when she acted in a movie based on her life in 1963.

Cleopatra was one of the most beautiful temptresses to ever walk the earth. She was bold, beautiful, and smart. But not all people agree that Cleopatra was beautiful. Some believe that she was more intelligent and shrewder than beautiful. There are many myths associated with the life of Cleopatra, which has made her life quite controversial. No one can say for sure whether she was beautiful or not.

But it does not matter whether Cleopatra was beautiful or not. What matters more is that she used her feminine charms and the power of seduction to seduce her way through difficulties. She wielded a lot of power, especially in a time when women were inferior to men. She was supposed to be extremely intelligent. She had a great voice and was knowledgeable about a lot of things. She was especially attractive and could subjugate anyone with her charms and wits. Even a dying man would become attracted to her charms.

Let us now have a look at the three things that every woman can learn from Cleopatra:

Tip 1

Look after yourself and care for yourself as well. Do not spend a lot of time grooming yourself. Instead, try to focus on your self-confidence and self-esteem. Nothing is sexier than a person who is bold and confident. Practice how to display your intelligence. It is also recommended to learn a few things about politics, power, and the potency of attraction. You need to understand the intricacies of life if you ever want to succeed. A woman who is bold and has a lot of confidence can take life by its horns and defeat it at its own game. Cleopatra was confident enough to seduce the most powerful man in the world. She not only seduced Julius Caesar but also bore him a son. She was able to do this based on her knowledge, her flirting skills, and, most important of all, her confidence. Without confidence, Cleopatra would have failed miserably and would have died at the hands of her brother.

Tip 2

Don't follow the rules to the T. Rules are meant to be broken, especially if they restrict you unjustly. You need to cultivate a sense of self-confidence. You need to find a new "self" that will be bolder, more confident, more stylish, and especially strong. Certain rules should be broken. Remember, flirting is supposed to be organic. You are trying to win over a man and not a machine. Instead of following all the rules carefully, break a few. If breaking the rules can help you get your man, then break them away.

For instance, the rules say that you must wait for the man to initiate the courtship. But if you believe that you can expedite the process, initiate the process of courtship yourself. Ultimately, it is all about getting your man to like you and make him attracted to you. All is well that ends well.

Tip 3

Always aim high. You need to put in a lot of energy into everything that you undertake. Never half-ass things. It is always better to put in your whole energy. Only serious efforts will lead you to success. Looks matter, but what matters more than looks is your confidence, your integrity, and your intellect. A generic looking smart person will always be more successful than a beautiful but dumb person.

Ultimately, Cleopatra has now become synonymous with beauty, but she was surely much more than that. If you want to mimic her, try to emulate her style, confidence, and intellect instead of focusing on her physical attributes. Her intellect will help you become a great flirter/ seductress.

Chapter Seven: Signs of High-Value Men (and Where to Find Them)

Many times, women are scared to approach men because they do not know whether the man they are interested in is worth approaching or not. Women love to date men who are "high value." They despise men who are ignorant, irritating, and crass. But understanding whether a man is high value or not can be quite complex. In this section, let us have a look at 20 things that all high-value men possess. If you find a man who possesses these qualities, then rest assured; he is a high-value man and a keeper as well.

He Commits to Himself and Others

A high-value man is committed to his life and his life goals. He will always work hard to make his life better. He will also work hard to make the life of his friends and girlfriend better. He considers his family, career, and life important. He knows what he can offer and will only approach a woman if he thinks she will be interested in him. He is not interested in anything vague. He likes being committed and will not falter at the sign of emotions.

He Makes an Effort

He puts a lot of effort into all the things that he does. This includes his wardrobe, his attire, his overall look, etc. He also pays close attention to what his woman wants. He never wants to fall short in front of his women. He is a master of detail. He likes everything done in a meticulous and bold manner. He will never ask a woman about what she wants to do because he knows what she likes and what she does not like. He knows how to please her. You will always feel safe and comfortable with a high-value man. He also puts in an effort in the bedroom as well. A high-value man is never satisfied unless his woman is satisfied. He wants to please his woman as much as he can. For him, the pleasure of his woman is the most important thing in the world.

He Makes Plans and Follows Through

A high-value man is good at making plans. He knows the value of time and will always have a busy schedule full of action and activity. He balances his personal as well as professional life properly. If he makes a plan, he will surely follow it through. So, if he plans a date with you, rest assured that he will make all the arrangements on time. If the date involves some form of activity, such as hiking or dancing, he will ask his date to pack her bag to fit the event. He likes to surprise his woman, but he does not want her to get caught out in an awkward situation.

He is a Great Conversationalist

A high-value man knows how to talk. He reads, he watches movies, he watches plays, and he attends seminars as well. He is a polymath and knows a lot of things, but he does not show it off all the time. He does not like to brag. His life is full of interesting experiences, and he has many stories to tell. He is open and is not scared to answer questions about himself. He displays an interest in his woman's life by asking are pertinent and relevant questions as well. He does not just care about her outer looks, for a high-value man, the insides count as well.

He Dresses and Grooms Himself Impeccably

A high-value man knows how to dress well and look dapper. This does not mean that he spends a lot of money on his clothes and attire. A person can look good and stylish without spending a lot of money. He spends time to care for himself. He understands style. He knows how to recreate the top designer looks for a fraction of the price. He would rather buy a large jacket and then tailor it to fit him properly. He goes to the gym and is fit. His shoes are always impeccable. He cuts his nails properly. He knows his colognes and wears them in the proper amount. He never overdoes anything. His hair is trimmed. His unwanted hair is either plucked or shaved or trimmed. This includes ear hairs, rogue eyebrow hairs, and nose hair as well. He understands that caring for yourself is a universal trait that members of all the genders must follow.

He Understands a Woman of Value

He understands that he cannot get everything he desires. He does not whine about rejection. He also does not start commenting about the woman who rejected him. He understands that attraction is a personal thing, and it is subjective to a lot of factors. He does not mind if a woman does not choose him. He will not give her a hard time just because she did not choose him. He will just wish her good luck and go on his way instead.

His Car and Home are Clean

A high-value man hates trash and junk. He believes that staying clean is an essential habit. He likes to keep his car and his house clean. He likes to maintain order in his home. Everything in his house is clean.

His bed is always made, his toilets are clean and fresh, his yard is never cluttered. He is meticulous about keeping things clean and tidy.

He's Fun!

A high-value man is aware that he is a funny and humorous person. A high-value man works hard, but he also plays hard. If someone is playing music and if the occasion is appropriate, he will surely dance. If there is a karaoke machine, he will be the first one to sing. He is a man who likes to live his life fully. Even if he is introverted, he will still have a lot of fun. He will also help others to have a lot of fun as well.

He's Clear On His Intentions

A high-value man is always clear with his intentions. You will never feel confused about him. He knows what he wants. He also knows what he can offer. He is there to offer you true love, if you are ready to reciprocate it. If he wants a committed relationship, he wants it to be perfect. A high-value man will always try to find a high-value woman, as well. He wants a woman who will not only encourage him but will inspire him as well. He wants a woman who adds to his life in a meaningful way. He wants a life partner who will help him follow his passions and dreams.

He Communicates Clearly

If a high-value man wants something, he will let you know it is a clear and efficient manner. If he does not like something about you, he will broach the subject in a diplomatic and professional way. He will never be crass or rude about anything. His goal is to reach an agreement and not to defeat others. If he ever feels that you are not ready to listen or hear his ideas, he will rather walk away than continue to talk to you.

He's Well Mannered

This is a given. A high-value man will always be well mannered. He will know how to eat at a fine dining restaurant. He will know what to do with a napkin while eating. He will always open the door for you and will offer you his hand. He will always put his hand on your back while leading you into a room. He will always hold your hand and carry it gracefully. If he must leave the table for a moment, he will get up and kiss you lightly. He never treats the wait staff, the valet, or the chauffeur rudely. For him, everyone is a human being who deserves respect and kindness.

He Shows the Right Amount of PDA

He knows when and how to show affection in public. He will never be crass about his display of affection.

He Seeks to Understand Women

A high-value man knows that no one is perfect in this world. He knows that people go through a lot of things in their day-to-day lives. A high-value man will always encourage a woman. He will help her rise, understand her heartbreak, and will always help her in all the walks of her life. He will help her follow her dreams. He will help her face her fears. He will help her accomplish things that she is capable of.

He understands and appreciates the beauty in chaos. He understands that life is not a piece of cake for everyone. Whenever he feels that his woman is feeling nervous or is sabotaging herself, he will help her see the light. He will help his woman to overcome her vulnerability and will help her grow as well. A high-value man knows that emotional bonding is far more crucial than physical bonding; he realizes that emotions are more important than sex or physical pleasure.

Therefore, it is clear that a high-value man is decent and bold. He is also charming and confident. Along with the above-mentioned qualities, there are many other qualities that a high-value man has. If a man possesses most of the qualities mentioned here, he is surely a high-value man; you should not let him get away!

Chapter Eight: The 21 Steps of Flirting

Flirting with a guy seems like an impossible task for many women because they find cute and hot men intimidating. Many women also have a constant fear of rejection, which they cannot ignore. But this does not mean that you should not try it! Flirting does not have to involve verbal actions; you can also flirt using a variety of gestures, expressions, and body language. Using these actions, you can even flirt across the room. A simple yet seductive smile, a bold hair flip, and an erotic look - all these are different ways of flirting with a man without using words. In-person you can flirt using various techniques as well. For instance, playful teasing, light touches, honest compliments are all different types of flirting techniques. You can even flirt using text messages. In this chapter, let us have a look at different types of flirting and how to use them.

For the convenience of the reader, this chapter has been divided into three sections:

Flirting From Across the Room

Let us first begin with the easiest types of all the three types of flirting: flirting from across the room.

Eye Contact

The importance of eye contact has been mentioned a few times in other chapters already. Eye contact is a great flirting technique that can be used at any time or any place. Eye contact is easy to do. You just need to do it in a limited amount, though. If you overdo it, you will end up looking like a creepy person who is obsessed with the man. Lingering eye contact is a great way to show that you are interested in someone. Eye contact is also a great test to check whether a man is interested in you or not. If you make eye contact with the guy and he holds eye contact, there are high chances that he is into you as well. But don't worry if he looks away, it is possible that he is shy and does not want to meet your eyes.

Another trick to check whether a guy is interested in you or not or when you want to display your interest is to look at the guy until he looks at you. Once he looks, just smile for a moment and look away. If you are feeling bold and cheeky, you can even throw in a wink to let your attraction be known.

Smiling

Another really simple way to display your interest is by smiling. According to many studies, smiling makes people seem more attractive. If you have beautiful teeth, flaunt them without any care.

Smiling makes people seem friendlier and happier as well. Smiling will make you look more approachable. If someone has a crush on you and he sees you smiling, he is more likely to come and greet you. If you act too grumpy, he will likely steer clear of you. Smiling also makes you feel happier. Happiness and confidence are the two keys to flirting. If you can flirt with confidence and a big smile on your face, you will seem attractive, and you will feel attractive as well.

Body Language

This is obvious; flirting requires the use of a lot of body moments and gestures. You cannot flirt properly without using body language. In fact, the flirting done with the help of bodily gestures is much more potent than that done with words. You don't even have to open your mouth to attract people and flirt with them. We have already covered two essential parts of body language for flirting, eye contact, and smiling, but there are other things that you should keep in mind as well.

Crossing Arms

Never cross your arms if you want to flirt with someone. Crossing arms is like the opposite activity to smiling. Smiling makes you seem happy, fun, and approachable while crossing your arms makes you seem like you are frustrated, angry, or cross. It will also scare him off because it makes you seem closed off and unapproachable. Some women (and men) tend to cross their arms when they are nervous. If you have the habit of doing this, pay close attention to it.

Flip Your Hair

Men love it when women flip her hair. Flipping hair is considered to be a very feminine and seductive action. It draws attention to your beautiful neck and to your long and pretty hair as well. It is also one of the best-known flirting techniques. So, if you want to flirt with a guy, just flip your hair in front of him- but don't be too obvious about it. There are other methods that you can use - for instance, playing with your hair is also a way to flirt with men.

Playing with Jewelry

Another common way to flirt with a man is to play with your jewelry. For instance, you can play with your necklace or pendant. This will draw his attention to your neckline. Men love the female neckline.

Get In His Way

Another really great way to flirt with a guy is to get in his path frequently. This does not mean that you should follow him or trouble him all the time. You just need to make some conscious effort to get into his path in a casual and nonchalant way. It should feel like destiny keeps on putting both of you around each other all the time. Do not be too obvious about this, or he will become suspicious.

If you work in the same office, walk around his desk a few times a day. If you both have dogs, take your dog to the same park where he walks his dog, etc. But don't overdo this. You don't want the guy to think that you are a stalker.

Look Your Best

This is quite obvious, but still, it needs to be said. Looking your best is essential if you want to feel confident and bold. It is necessary to look your best whenever your crush is around you. Looking your best does not mean that you should go around looking like a sleazy woman. Similarly, it does not mean going around in evening gowns all the time. You just need to dress carefully in clean and proper clothes. You just need to be well-groomed and dressed in a neat manner. If you look at your best, you will feel your best. If you feel confident about your looks, you will feel confident about flirting as well.

Here are some tips that can help you look your best:

• Keep your hair washed and clean regularly. It should always feel smooth and smell fresh.

• Brush your teeth. Your teeth do not need to be "fake" white.

• Shave around parts you find unfeminine.

• Make yourself pretty. This step includes a lot of things. For instance, if you like painting your nails, paint them. If you like wearing a lot of jewelry, wear it, etc.

• Wear clean clothes. Avoid dressing like a slob. Your clothes should be comfortable.

• Try different hairstyles. It should look like you put in some effort in your everyday look. You can also try out different hair colors. But don't overdo this, or it will do a lot of damage to your hair.

First Move

Traditionally men are supposed to make the first move, and it is recommended to wait if you can for him to take the initiative. But if you feel that it is becoming too much and that you cannot wait, it is time to take things into your own hands. Waiting for men to begin the pursuit is a boring and cumbersome task. If you get fed up with it, it is time to approach him on your own.

Flirting in Person

Talking

While body language is a great way to flirt with men, using your verbal prowess can help you get ahead of everyone. It can allow you to flirt in a far more open and involved way. Talking to your crush can help you tell him about a lot of things and express a lot of ideas that cannot be expressed using your body language. Talking to a crush is easy if you know what to talk about. If you don't, then some common topics on which you can talk about include recent events, school, work, etc.

Another great way to open a conversation is with the help of a question. Open your conversation with a question he will be forced to answer. Asking a question also shows that you are interested in a person and are not just interested in talking to yourself. You can ask him about some recent events, the latest books, the latest movies, etc. You can also ask him about what he did over the weekend.

It is recommended to avoid asking questions that can be answered in one word. For instance, do not ask him questions such as "Do you like this actor?" or "Is this your favorite book?" etc. If you ask such questions, then the conversation will surely die out as these are simple yes or no questions.

Another tip to get him talking is switching the conversation. Who does not love talking about themselves? Try to talk to him about things that he seems to be passionate about. These subjects will surely get him talking. For instance, if he loves sports, you can talk to him about sports as well.

Tip: While talking, it is recommended to use his name a lot. People love to hear their names being used by others, especially in a conversation, and especially when the opposite sex uses it. Calling your crush by his name is a great way to make him interested in you. It will also help you to create a sense of intimacy and affection.

Smile and Laugh

While we have already covered smiling, this kind of smiling is different. Smiling and laughing while you are talking to a person is different from smiling from a distance. Smiling throughout the conversation is important, as it will help you let your beau know that you like him and that you feel comfortable around him. He should understand that you like what he is saying that you enjoy his voice. Laughing and smiling frequently will also make you look attractive. It will make you seem like a fun-loving, happy, and cheerful person.

Laughing at a man's jokes is a great way to make him feel confident and bold. Men love to be funny, and they appreciate it when members of the opposite sex laugh at their jokes. If you do not like his jokes, just give a genuine courtesy laugh. Remember, do not cackle like a hag, or he will be scared out of his wits.

Touching

Communication is not just verbal. To enhance the intensity of verbal communication, it is necessary to get physical as well. Find ways in which you can touch your crush from time to time. This touch does not need to be too physical. A simple brush of fingers or a graze of the arm is enough. Touching your crush frequently is a great way to let your crush know that you are flirting with him. It will show him that you are willing to get physical. Here are some tips that can help you with this step:

Touch His Forearm Gently When You Are Talking

When he cracks a joke that you find funny, reach out and touch his arm while laughing. You can also do this while consoling him. Put your elbow or arm on his casually. This will create a feeling of camaraderie between the both of you. It will also prove that you feel comfortable around him. While walking together, lean into him "accidentally." If you are flirty enough, brush your hand against his hand and wait for his reaction.

Another way to flirt with a man is by straightening his collar. To do this, just tell him that his collar is crooked and fix it for him. You can do this without telling him. Just stand in front of him, look into his eyes, and straighten his collar gently. While doing this, brush your fingers gently across his neck. Once done, just look into his eyes and say, "Hmm, now that looks better" and gently back away.

Your Body

Men are visual beings. They understand things better when they are shown. They love when they get sneak peeks of your body here and there. This is a great way to let him know that you are attracted to him. To do this, just subtly draw his attention to your body from time to time. This will get his heart racing. It will also force him to conclude that he is interested in you. Below are some tricks that can help you.

One of the easiest ways to display your body is to ask the man whether you should get a belly button piercing. To do this, just pull up your top slightly and show him your belly button. Ask him whether it would look good or not. If he starts to stammer, well done, you have successfully caught his attention.

Pretend that you have some shoulder pain and that you would like a massage. Pull down your neckline slightly to show your skin. If you are lucky, he will give you a simple massage.

Lips work great for seduction and flirting. Lick your lips from time to time. This will make him think about kissing. You can also bite them, lick them, or apply some lipstick to draw his attention toward your lips. Do remember to be subtle while doing this!

It is recommended to do this in a limited way. Do not overdo it and always use these techniques in moderation. If you overdo them, he will think that you are desperate. If you are not on a beach, don't show up in a bikini. Remember, you want to attract a high-value man - not a sleazebag.

Dance

Dancing is one of the primal forms of attracting a mate. Dancing with him is a fun way to let your guy know that you like him. Dancing does not need to be too serious. You can dance anywhere; it does not matter. The only thing that matters is that you get some quality, one-on-one time with him.

It is recommended to make it obvious that you plan to choose him to dance with. Pull his hand and take him away from his group of friends. If he lets you take him away, then rest assured, he likes you as well. Sexy dancing is fine too! But do not overdo it. Do not be overtly sexual, and do not do dance styles such as grinding. It will make him uncomfortable, especially if there are people around him.

If your guy does know how to dance or is an awkward (or an outright bad) dancer, then it is your duty to make him feel comfortable. You can do this by slowly easing him into the dance, or you can join him by making some wacky moves as well. Just be sure that he does not feel mocked. If you can make him laugh, he will surely enjoy your company.

It is recommended to ease him into slow dancing as well. Slow dancing is sexy, seductive, and full of passion and romance. Look into his eyes while you are dancing. It will melt him like a chocolate bar.

Pay Him a Compliment

Many women think that only men are supposed to pay compliments. But this is a myth. Guys appreciate compliments too. In fact, everyone likes getting compliments. Appreciating your crush is a great way to show him that you like him. He will appreciate the interest that you are showing in him. He will also think that you are paying attention to him. If you do not know how to compliment men, check out the list, below, of things you can try!

Be Specific

Compliments need to be specific and personal. Generic compliments such as "You look great," "You look hot," "You are cute," are nice, but they are common. They are generic. He must have heard them before. He won't remember them. To make your compliment count, it is recommended to compliment him about something specific, like a specific trait or quirk. The compliment needs to be fresh. He will surely remember your compliment. One great way to make your compliment seem personal is by complimenting the color of his eyes. This works on dual levels because it allows you an excuse to gaze into his eyes for a long time.

Profession or Hobby

Compliment him about his work or hobby. For instance, if he paints, compliment his paintings. Make the compliments genuine by studying art.

Voice

When you compliment him, lower your voice slightly and lean into him. If possible, compliment him in a whispered or husky tone. Your compliment should seem like a secret or something intimate.

Eye Contact

It is recommended to make eye contact while paying him a compliment. You can also add a tiny smile with this. This will prove that you are genuinely impressed and that you are paying him a sincere compliment.

Do not go overboard with compliments. If you compliment him a lot, it will seem fake. It will reduce the impact of your compliments. He may even think that you are pranking him. A few sincere compliments are far better than dozens of fake ones.

Playfully Tease Him

Playful teasing and humor are two great flirting techniques. You just need to be careful while using them, though. Teasing is great because it creates a feeling of intimacy. It also proves to the man that you have a sense of humor. But remember, if you deal it out, you should be able to accept teasing from him as well.

Tease your man about trivial things. For instance, if you are in school, tease him, saying that he has a crush on a teacher. If he is a dog person, tell him that he loves his dog more than any other human being.

If he is good looking, jest around and ask him how his Abercrombie job is going. If he just came back from a gym, make a hyperbolic statement about his muscles. Remember not to be offensive. Never get too personal while teasing your guy. You do not want to create any misunderstandings. Never insult his appearance, his family, his friends, or his career. You do not want to alienate him.

Leave Him Wanting More

If you ever feel the conversation has started to drag on for too long, or that he appears to be distracted or bored, then walk away as soon as you can. Your conversation should never seem boring. It is better to leave while he is still interested. This will leave him wanting more.

Create an opening for the next time. Instead of dragging up an old topic, just move away quickly. Promise him that you will continue with the topic the next day.

Another trick to drive men crazy is by leaning in for a kiss and then at the last moment turning your head just to whisper a compliment in his ear.

Flirting Over Text

Text Him "Accidentally"

If you aren't sure how to initiate a conversation, you can do it by texting him by accident. To do this, you need to pretend that you were trying to text someone else but accidentally texted him instead. You can send a text like, "Oh, you are so right, but whatever, come on! Let us meet!" After a couple of minutes, message him saying, "Oh, I am sorry, the wrong person!" He will surely text you next and will start a conversation with you.

Don't Be Boring

Text messages can get boring quickly, especially if you send pointless things such as "What's up?" etc. Texts like these are highly uninteresting and boring. They will not take you far with your crush. It is recommended to be as unique as possible. Send a message only if you think that he will find it interesting. For instance, let him know about things that remind you of him, as this is a great way to initiate a conversation.

Leave Some Questions Hanging

Don't be too eager while texting. You do not need to respond to every message. You do not want to seem too eager, or he will think that you are under his control. It is recommended to respond to only a couple of things and leave some questions hanging. This will allow you to have a sense of mystery. Similarly, it will help you create a sense of passion around you, as well. It is also recommended to give him some breathing space. Do not ask him a lot of questions all at once. He should not feel hassled or bombarded with questions. It is recommended to keep the messages as short as possible. The messages should be sweet, simple, and quick.

Be Suggestive

Once both of you get comfortable with texting, it is now time to make things more interesting. A lot of simple texting will make things bland and clichéd. You need to add some passion to the texts. Things should start to heat up. You need to drop some hints to say that you are interested in becoming more than friends.

It is recommended to play safely in the beginning. Do not send messages that are too racy or sexy messages in the beginning. He will think that you are too sleazy. You can keep things sexy and cute simultaneously. For instance, send him a sultry flirting text. If he responds in the same tone, it is time to pull out the big guns. Pay him a flirty comment or compliment him. You can compliment him about his body etc.

You can be even racier by suggesting some suggestive things. For instance, you can send him a text saying that you are in the shower. Don't say anything after that, and let him imagine things on his own.

Don't Send Too Many Texts

While texting is a great way to flirt, you should never overdo it. According to the rules of texting, you are supposed to send only the number of texts that you receive. If you send a few more, then it will come off as desperation. For instance, if you send your crush 20-30 texts a day and he only responds to 3-5 of them, then you are certainly overdoing it.

You need to practice self-control, or you will come off as creepy. Do not text all the time; instead, wait for him to reply. Do not text until you have something interesting to say. If you do not have anything important to say, do not say anything. If you have sent more than two texts and have not received a reply, then it is time to stop and wait.

Similarly, it is always better to wait for a guy to send you a text. Be mysterious and bold. Act kind of aloof for a while. If he texts you, he is surely interested in you. Never send messages such as "lol" and "k" etc. These texts are atrocious because they disallow any chance to continue the conversation. They are also a pet peeve of many people. Many people find them extremely obnoxious.

Picture Text

Texting images is a great option for communication. This way, your crush will always have your picture on his phone.

You can send him a group picture with your friends and ask him to join you. Or you can send a random selfie and ask him to entertain you. You can even send him a movie poster and ask him whether he would like to go out to a movie.

Make a Date

Texting can be used to make plans, as well. For instance, if you want to ask the guy for a date but are too nervous about doing so face-to-face, you can do it in the text as well. Just send him the movie poster as mentioned above and ask him whether he would like to join you.

If he says yes- congratulations, you have a date on your hands. Now go and plan it!

If he says no, that's fine; just say, "Cool! Some other time then." It is quite easy to play cool over text. It is not as nerve-wracking as in real life.

Therefore, these are some of the main techniques and methods of flirting with the man of your dreams, as these steps are easy and quick. You just need to be cautious of one thing, though. Never overdo these things, or else your beau will think that you are desperate and are being creepy.

Chapter Nine: Seductive Body Language Techniques

In the last chapter, we saw a lot of flirting techniques that can be used to attract a man. We also covered flirting with the help of body language. But there is much more to body language than what meets the eye. In this chapter, let us have a look at some of the most common techniques that can help you to flirt with your beau.

Before moving onto the intricacies of body language and how to use it to attract and flirt with your guy, it is necessary to understand what body language is.

What is Body Language?

As the name suggests, body language means the various movements, gestures, and expressions that your body does. It is literally talking through your body. Every person uses their body to send signals to other people. These signals are varied and convey a lot of different emotions. For instance, these signals can convey messages and feelings such as repulsion, attraction, insecurity, security, annoyance, and happiness as well. It depends on the position and movement of your body parts what message you want to convey. Many times, it is simple to convey your message through your body or body language more than your words. For instance, when you are annoyed at a person or do not like whatever he is saying, you automatically cross your arms in front of you. Some people also tap their feet when they are impatient. Therefore, even though you are not aware of it, you are communicating your feelings effectively.

Along with the above feelings, body language can also convey other feelings, including love and affection. For instance, if you are interested in a man, you automatically lean towards him while talking. You may even start to mirror his actions. Your mind may not accept that you like him, but your body certainly knows that you are totally into him. You can use body language for your own benefit. Your body is a great tool to seduce men. You just need to know how to do it and what to do it.

Tips on How to Seduce Men with Body Language

In this section, let us have a look at some of the easiest and common body language tips that you can use to flirt with a guy. These are great for general seduction as well. How you use these tips depends on you.

Use Your Smile

Everyone is born with a great smile. And everyone likes to see a smiling person as well. A smile is a potent asset to attract people. How you smile and use it matters a lot. There are two kinds of smiles, the "Pan Am Smile," and the "Duchenne smile." You are supposed to use the Duchenne smile and not the Pan Am smile. Pan Am smile, as the name suggests, is the smile that air hostesses use. It is a fake smile that has no emotions behind it. The Duchenne smile is a genuine smile. You are supposed to smile with your eyes while smiling the Duchenne smile. When you smile genuinely, your partner will think that you are really into him.

Another form of the smile is the sexy smile. A sexy smile can be used to let your partner know that you are available and that you would like to do some naughty things with him.

Use Your Belly Button

This might seem strange, but it is true. You can use your belly button to communicate with the guy you like.

According to researchers, pointing your belly button toward the person you love shows that you are interested in him. It also shows that you trust this person. Therefore, even if your head is turned away, it is recommended to keep your belly button toward him.

Touch Him...But Not Too Much

Some slight touching is appropriate and needs to be done to show that you are genuinely interested in the guy. But if you keep on touching the guy all the time, he will find it inappropriate. He may even get creeped out. Keep things as "accidental" as possible. Never forget that you are supposed to be tasteful. Always do things in a subtle way.

Avoid Crossing Your Arms

Crossing your arms is a negative signal that you send toward people you dislike. If you cross your arms while talking to the guy you like, he will subconsciously think that you don't like him. Crossing your arms shows that you are not interested in the person. It also shows that you are disconnected from the present and are not interested in anything that is going on around you. Crossing your arms frequently can also show that you are insecure about something.

Strike a Power Pose

Power poses are not limited only to businessmen and women. Power poses allow you to bring your best side forward. The people who use high power poses such as hands-on-hips etc. feel more confident than people who use low power poses. People who use high-power poses tend to perform better in their day-to-day lives. This strategy can also be used while flirting. Spread your legs, keep your shoulder back, and put your hands on your hips while talking to a man. This will make you seem strong and bold.

Lock Eyes with Him and Then Look Away

It has already been mentioned that eyes are quite important if you want to learn how to flirt properly. Batting of eyes, coy eyes, eye contact, etc. are all flirting techniques that are heavily dependent on eyes. When talking to regular people such as your parents, or your neighbors, or your friend, you tend to make eye contact for a minute and then look away. This is normal. But when you want to convey your emotions and feelings of attraction, the eye contact needs to be more intense. It needs to be deeper. Don't be shy about making eye contact with the person you are interested in.

Only eye contact is not important. You also need to learn how and when to lower your eyes. Once you maintain significantly long eye contact, look down gently and part your lips slightly. This is a highly erotic move that will heat up the room. It mimics the expressions that women tend to have while having an orgasm.

Make the Most of Your Lips

After your eyes, your lips are the most important organ for flirting and seducing a man. There are many things that you can do with your lips to seduce a man. The first thing that you need to do is to wear bold colors - the bolder the color, the better the attraction. Red is the color of passion and love. But if you feel uncomfortable using a stark red lipstick, you can use a slightly subtle shade. Biting, opening them slightly, parting, batting them, are some of the many things that you can do with your lips to attract the attention of the guy you like.

Play with Your Hair to Attract Him

While hair is dead, it can surely help passion for coming alive. There are many ways to use hair to attract the attention of a man. You can:

- Toss your hair back.
- Pull it over one should while exposing your neck.
- Putting it up when he is around
- Twirling a section around your finger.
- Pick a couple of tactics and do them, but don't go overboard. It will look strange.

Show Him Your Interest Using Facial Expressions

You will be shocked to know that a person makes about 25,000 expressions throughout the day on an average. Faces are extremely expressive, and you can use them to communicate a lot of things. Sometimes your face can communicate a lot better than your voice can. You need to learn how to use your face to tell him what is on your mind.

Lean in Toward Him

Leaning towards a person shows that you are interested in him or her. When you lean towards a guy, he will think that you are interested in him and that you want to talk to him. Leaning away from someone shows that you are not interested in them at all.

Therefore, whenever he is talking, lean in slightly. His subconscious will pick the signal, and he will realize that you are interested in him.

Wear Clothes That Make You Feel Your Best

One of the best things that you can do to make your body language attractive is by being as comfortable as possible. If you are comfortable with yourself, others will feel comfortable about you as well. Therefore, if you do not normally flip your hair and feel uncomfortable about doing it, it is recommended to avoid it altogether. Instead, do something else that you are comfortable with. The same is the case with your clothes. Many times, people think that looking sexy on the first date is essential. But if you feel uncomfortable in your clothes, it will backfire hilariously.

Instead of wearing excessively skimpy and tight clothes, it is recommended to wear clothes that are clean, fit you well, and have no wrinkles. A tiny bit of cleavage is fine, but do not overdo it. Remember, you are supposed to be attractive and not sleazy.

Your clothes can make you look sexy, but nothing is sexier than a lot of self-confidence. So instead of focusing a lot on your clothes, focus on cultivating self-confidence instead.

Live In the Moment

While it is true that these tips can help you immensely while flirting and seducing people, you should not limit yourself to them. Flirting and seduction are not mechanical, they are organic, and they need to be changed according to the place and time. These tips should be used as a script for your date. Treat these tips as suggestions. You can change and adapt them according to your discretion. Honestly, if you are confident and bold enough, you can change these tips and make them suitable for you.

You cannot prepare a blueprint for a date. It will always be unpredictable. Therefore, change your strategy accordingly.

Ultimately, every woman has a different method and approach towards seduction and flirting. Every woman uses her body differently, making body language a highly individualistic subject. For instance, some women use dance to seduce men, while others use their voices. If you cannot use any of these two, then you can surely use yours. Whatever technique you use, remember to personalize it according to your needs. It is necessary to be as authentic as possible. Only authenticity will produce good results, so be authentic.

It is also recommended to think of the things that you want from the man you are trying to seduce. Do not use these steps if you are in a new relationship and are still treading the waters. If you use these tips in the initial stages of a new relationship, the guy will think that you are interested in casual hookups only.

Chapter Ten: The Official First Date - The Major Dos and Don'ts

The modern world is incredibly rapid and is like a whirlwind. Everything is fast-paced, and every new day brings in a new challenge. It has become quite difficult to find the right person. But this does not mean that the modern world has not come up with modern solutions to solve these problems.

For instance, nowadays, there are many events such as singles nights, speed-dating events, etc. that can help you find the one. The time at such events is limited. This limited time, combined with the hardships of the world, can make it quite difficult to find the right one. It is therefore recommended to be your best self all the time. You need to put your best foot forward all the time. You need to be in your top form.

First dates can be quite difficult. There are many things that you should avoid while going on a first date. Similarly, there are many things that you must follow while going on a first date. In this chapter, let us have a look at some of the most common factors that you need to consider for making your first date a successful one. If you follow these tips carefully, you will surely be able to make your first date count.

Do's

Turn Up On Time

It pays to be on time, especially on first dates. Being late is a sign of tardiness. It also shows that you do not care about the date. Every minute of delay will make your date think that you have stood them up. Sitting alone and waiting in a restaurant or a café is a traumatic experience. No one likes to go through this experience. Therefore, it is recommended to be on time. If you cannot be on time, inform your date of the potential delay.

Display Interest

First dates are difficult because you are bombarded with a lot of information. Do not expect to remember all this information. Some of the information may be relevant to you, but most of it won't be relevant or important. But this does not mean that you should not act like you are interested in the information. Feigning interest is a characteristic that everyone needs to learn. If a man puts in an effort to show that he is interested in you and talks to you about his life, then it is recommended to show at least some amount of interest in what he is saying. Even if the topic bores you to death, pay attention to him. Don't yawn!

Listen More

Everyone loves to talk about themselves. People can spend hours on end talking about themselves. People tend to do this a lot on the first date because they want to prove that they are indeed a catch. But this constant verbal diarrhea will bore anyone. Similarly, it won't help you in the long-term. A first date is an opportunity to find out things about your date. So instead of talking a lot, try to listen a lot as well. Speak less, listen more to show that you are genuinely interested in the person.

Ask Questions

If you ever feel that the conversation is entering the "silent" territory, ask him questions. The questions should be lighthearted and interesting. The questions should be asked in a way to ensure descriptive answers. Remember, asking questions does not mean interrogation. Do not ask any personal questions about your date. Similarly, avoid topics that can lead to controversies. If your date refuses to answer a question, do not force him to answer it.

Make Eye Contact

Eye contact is quite sexy if you know how to do it. Eyes are windows to a person's soul. They show your real selves. You can convey a lot of feelings such as love, honesty, and attraction through eyes. Dishonest people tend to avoid looking at people in their eyes. If you do not look into the eyes of your date, he will think that you are lying or are being dishonest. Maintaining eye contact is essential if you want to create a spark of chemistry between you. But making eye contact does not mean that you need to stare at your date all the time. Maintaining good eye contact means looking away from time to time. If you keep on staring at your date, he will find it creepy.

Be Honest

Relationships are built on trust and honesty. You cannot expect a relationship to work if you are not honest. It is recommended to be as honest as possible. Random fakery and falsifications will not work, and your lies will be exposed eventually. You should always be proud of who you are and what you are. If your date does not like something about you or vice versa, it is better to be honest on the first date itself instead of lamenting later.

Make an Offer to Pay the Bill

According to the unwritten rules of chivalry (which some men and women still follow), it is the duty of a man to pay the bill. But this is a dated and sexist concept. Instead of forcing your date to pay for you, it is recommended to offer to pay. Show your intent to pay the bill. Many men find this sexy because it shows that you can care for yourself and that you are confident and bold. If he insists on paying the bill, accept it graciously.

Compliments

There is no one in this world who does not like a compliment. While men often pay compliments to women, it is recommended to throw in a couple of compliments towards men as well. Compliments can change the tone of the conversation. They can make the conversation highly positive. It is recommended to keep compliments simple and clean. Say things like you mean them. Fake compliments will not be appreciated. Do not compliment your date just because he complimented you.

Don'ts

Let us now have a look at some of the don'ts of first dates.

Don't Talk About How Great You Are

Talking about yourself and how great you are is off-putting. No one wants to hear you talk about yourself all the time. It is true that the first date is an opportunity to talk about yourself, but it is also an opportunity to get to know your date. If you keep on talking, without giving your date any chance to speak, he will feel disinterested and frustrated. If you want the conversation to be successful, both the partners should be involved equally. Whenever you feel that you are talking a lot, take a step back and let your date speak. Remember, speak less and listen more.

Don't Keep Checking Your Phone

One of the rudest things that you can do while talking to someone is checking your phone all the time. Being on the phone all the time while someone else is talking to you is rude. It will make the person feel that you are not interested in them or are being disrespectful towards them. If you keep on checking your phone all the time, your date will think that your phone is more important than them. If you are indeed expecting an urgent call, it is recommended to let your date know about this. He will surely understand.

Don't Be Under-Dressed

It is far better to be slightly overdressed than to be underdressed. Showing up to the date, looking like a hobo, will kill all your chances of a second date. Look fresh and active. Your date will surely appreciate your looks. Showing up for the date in sweats shows that you do not care for the date and therefore did not put in any effort.

The Myth of Perfection

One of the biggest myths in the world is "perfection." No one is perfect, and you should not try to be perfect, either. It is recommended to focus on the relationship instead of focusing on how to appear perfect. Your date will surely accept you with your quirks. Truly, imperfection makes a person perfect.

Past Relationships

Many people tend to spend a lot of time talking about their past relationships on their first date. While you should never hide your past, you should dwell on it either. No one wants to hear how much you loved your ex or how much he cheated on you. If you ever find yourself in such a situation, it is recommended to change the subject as soon as possible.

Don't Think Too Far Ahead

We get it, you are looking for commitment, but this does not mean that you start planning your whole life with your date just after the first meeting. Instead of focusing on what can happen, try to focus on the current moment itself. Focus on the present and try to focus on connecting with him. Live in the moment and be happy in it.

Don't Use Cheesy Lines

Cheesy lines never work. Only horny teenagers use them, and the only place where they seem to work is shown and in the movies. They are crass, stupid, and immature. Instead of throwing cheesy lines at your date, try to develop a personality. Read more, watch more movies, and indulge yourself in various activities. These things are far better than cheesy pickup lines.

Therefore, as first dates can be a piece of cake, if you know what to do and what to avoid, this list will surely help you crack the code of perfect first dates.

Chapter Eleven: Kissing - Are You Doing It Right?

One of the most intimate, erotic, and passionate things that you can do with your partner is kissing. Kissing displays your passion, your love, and your affection. Kissing can also be quite sensual and erotic. There are many different types of kisses and kisses. The basic difference between kisses is a simple kiss and a passionate kiss. You can take your making out experience to the next level by making your regular kisses passionate. In this section, let us have a look at some interesting tips that will your kissing experience more passionate and bolder.

Stay in the Moment

A kiss does not work just on the physical level. A kiss can only become passionate when both the partners are fully present in the moment. The intentions, ideas, and thoughts of both the partners are crucial to making a kiss successful. A kiss is complete on its own, and it should be treated like this. It is recommended to be fully present in the moment. You should not use kissing as a jumping platform for other activities. Never rush into or rush out of kissing. Your kissing should open your heart to your partner. He should feel the love and emotions seeping through the kiss. A passionate kiss should be able to display how much you love him and how attracted you are to him.

Do not be overwrapped with the notion of kissing. Be mindful of whatever you are doing, but don't let kissing become too mechanical. Kissing is an activity of passion; it does not have to be a calculated activity. If you are thinking about anything else, stop it. Just focus on your object of attraction and dive deep into the kiss.

It's More than the Lips

Many people think that lips and tongue are the two organs that are involved in kissing. While this is technically true, kissing that involves only these two organs is often bland and lacks passion and intensity. To make kisses more intense and passionate, you need to involve a lot of things in the process of kissing. It is true that your lips do most of the work while kissing, but to make the process more passionate, you can mix in some sensual touches. This will heat up the room. You can also touch your partner's chin or play with his earlobes. Make them kiss as "full-bodied" as possible. You can also moan while kissing to make things more intense.

Keep Things Loose

As said above, kissing should not become a task or a mechanical process. You need to let loose and enjoy it as much as you can. Kissing should involve a lot of tongue. The tongue is highly flexible and strong. You can make it move around and tighten it at the correct places to make the feelings intense. Your passion should flow like an uninhibited stream and should drench each other. Enjoy the unending river of pleasure and ride its waves with full force.

Eye Contact is Your Friend

Eye contact can be incredibly sexy if you know how to do it. Look into your partner's eyes while approaching the kiss. This will help you convey your passion to him. Once the kissing starts, shut your eyes and enjoy the waves of pleasure.

Test the Waters with the Tongue

Sometimes, some people like the use of tongues while kissing. If your partner is one of these guys, then ask him whether he would like to use his tongue while kissing. If he agrees, use it gradually. It needs to be slow. Do not force him. Ask him from time to time whether he likes it, whether he enjoys it, and whether he finds it pleasurable. Kissing should feel natural. Pay close attention to the body language of your partner and check whether he is comfortable or not. Try to match the pace of your partner. If he is moaning with pleasure, pull him in, and do not stop. If you feel him pulling back, then slow down slightly.

Build Energy Slowly

Keep things slow! Pausing from time to time between kissing can really make things more intense. These pauses can help you convey your passion. It also provides your lips and tongue a moment of respite. Look into his eyes deeply and build up the passion for your next kiss. The slow nature of kisses will only heat things up. Gently grazing his thighs while kissing can help you make things move in the right direction.

Study Up

While it may seem hilarious, studying before kissing can really help you make your kisses passionate. There are many online tutorials, books, TV shows, movies, etc. available that can help you learn how to kiss. Pay close attention to the details and list down what you find attractive. It can be the movements, gestures, eye contact, etc. Use these details when you kiss your partner the next time.

Practice as Much as Possible

The best way to become a passionate and sensual kisser is by experimenting and practicing a lot. You can do solo practice, or you can find a partner to practice as well. For solo practice, just emulate your kiss on the back of your hand. This will help you to learn how to use your lips, your tongue, and your mouth. You need to be as confident as possible with your technique. But don't forget the passion. A kiss needs both passion and confidence to make it a great kiss.

Kissing is an essential aspect of any romantic relationship. While everyone knows how to kiss, not everyone knows how to do it correctly. You need to do it properly to make things passionate and intense. This chapter will surely help you become a great and passionate kisser.

Chapter Twelve: How to Lure Him into Bed (in a Non-Slutty Way)

Is there a man that you have been eyeing up for a long time? Are you attracted to him but do not know how to approach him? Do you drool at the prospect of getting him into your bed? But are you scared because you do not know how to do so? Then don't worry. This chapter will help you unlock the secrets of getting a guy into your bed without acting slutty or sleazy.

Approaching a man for sex is not difficult. You just need to understand the intricacies and nuances of the art of seduction. It is not rocket science. It is quite easy. You just need to be confident, bold, and strong; everything else will work for you just fine.

Here are some easy to follow tips that will help you learn how to pull a man into your bed. These tips will put you on the right track towards your dream guy. Remember, these tips are a form of guide for you. You need to put in the details according to your needs and requirements, as well as the circumstances.

Don't Be Too Eager

There are proper times and places for everything. Do not be too eager to lure your man into bed. If you feel that things are mellow and cold, you should refrain from approaching the dream guy. No one likes people who are too into them. If you appear too creepy, clingy, or "horny," your dream guy will think that you are a freak, and he will run away. Men love the feeling of the chase. They love the adrenaline rush. They want women to play a little hard to get. They want you to make them envious. Men dislike women who come onto them all the time. A little chase will boost their ego and will always help you to get him in your bed.

Feel Sexy

To be sexy, you need to feel sexy. Sexiness is attractive. It attracts people toward you like a magnet. Sexiness is not related to your beauty; it is much more than that. If you are confident about your sexiness, you will ooze it. Think about your best features whenever you approach someone. You need to feel sexy to act sexy and be sexy as well. Your sexiness should be so seductive that every guy you approach should want you. You should be able to feel desirable all the time.

Be Flirty

Flirting is a great way to show a guy that you are interested in him. You need to tease the guy and make him jealous. Do not be obvious about your attraction toward him. Your attraction should never be obvious. He should feel that you are interested in him, but the interest is temporary. If a guy ever thinks that you are in his control, he will stop caring about you. Your chances to get into his pants will become negligible. He will make you his plan B. You should never become someone's plan B.

Focus on Building the Tension

Sexual tension is essential if you ever want to sleep with your dream guy. This can only be achieved with the help of various gestures and body language. Stand close to him whenever you want to talk to him. While talking casually, brush your arm against his. Expose a side of your neck by putting your hair to one side casually. Whenever he makes you laugh, touch him gently. These are some of the most potent ways to build sexual tension. What we say with our words matters, but what we say with our bodies matters more. Let your body do the talking for you.

Don't Hang Around

If you are at a bar or at a club and your dream guy approaches, then have a casual chat with him. But do not tail him throughout the night. It is true that you do not want him to go home with anyone else, but if you follow him around all the time, it will make you seem creepy. Similarly, it will prove that you have your eyes set on him. This will reduce his interest in you. To avoid this, enjoy your night. Dance with your friends. You need to show your beau that you do not need him; rather, he needs you.

Make Him Compete

This means that you need to show him that there are other men who are interested in you. Men love to chase and compete. Show him that he is not the only one who is after you. If he approaches you, greet him casually, and indulge in small talk. In this conversation, point out how other men are interested in you. This needs to be done in a diplomatic and subtle way. If you act too harshly, it will ruin your chances forever.

Create an Opportunity for Him to Approach You

Men do not like approaching women when they are surrounded by people or are in a group. It is quite an intimidating task to approach a group of women, especially if they are confident and sexy. If you are with your group all the time, your dream boy will never approach you. To prevent this, go to the bar alone and have a drink. You can also dance alone, away from your group for a while. Allow him some space to approach you on his own.

Make Eye Contact

Eye contact is incredibly sexy and bold. It is one of the best ways to flirt. Make and maintain eye contact with your dream boy from time to time. Do not overdo it; just a couple of times is fine as well. When men look at women, the first thing they notice is their face. They do this so that they can check whether a woman is interested in them or not. Eye contact is the best way to let your man know that you are indeed interested and want him as soon as possible.

Don't Give Him Everything

So, you did manage to get him in the bed? Congratulations! But wait! Do not hurry. It is understandable that now that you finally have your dream guy in your bed, you just want to rip off his clothes and have a passionate night of lovemaking. But if you do this, he will not come back for more. If you are making out passionately, pull back from time to time. This will help you enhance the passion and the intensity of the moment. He becomes enraged with passion, and his desires will become bolder. This will surely make him come back for more all the time.

Use Texting to Your Advantage

If your dream guy asks for your number or if you have text in the past, then you are on the right track. Texting may seem to be a bland form of communication, but it can be incredibly sexy and naughty as well. If you really want to get the guy in your bed, just be naughty and a little cheeky. Tell him what you are wearing or let him know what you want him to do. Let him visualize what he would like to do with you. This method can be used when he is around you or is far away from you. It will drive him crazy with passion.

But Don't Over Text

Remember, men love the chase. If you act too sleazy and desperate by texting him all the time, his interest in you will wane quickly. Let him make the first move, even if you desperately want to get into his bed. He should feel the same desperation that you are experiencing. If you have sexted in the past, pull back and act friendly. Play it cool for some time. He will put in more effort, which will make the whole thing sexier.

The Yes Game

If he does decide to make love to you, then brilliant! But wait; don't say yes right away. Remember, men love the chase, and now that he has approached you with his intentions, he is under your power now. You need to learn how to control him now. Play hard to get to make things even tenser. Do not give him whatever he wants right away. Enhance the sexual tension to make lovemaking even more passionate.

If You Just Met Him, Don't Text Him

If you have just met your dream guy at a party and you exchanged numbers, let him make the first move. Do not call him or text him either. If he is really interested in you, he will surely text you first. Remember, men love the chase. Be nonchalant about things and let him do things at his own pace.

These tips have been tried and tested. They will surely help you get your dream man in your bed in no time. Just remember to keep things classy and not act desperate. Save the sluttiness for the bedroom, please!

Chapter Thirteen: When Flirting Goes Wrong

Flirting is a great way to attract the attention of the person you like. While flirting is generally harmless, it can lead to some problems if it is not done correctly. In this chapter, let us have a look at specific issues that are associated with dating and flirting.

Internal Dating Obstacles

Many times, singles complain a lot about a lot of external factors that they find problematic about dating. These include weird dates, weird ideas as presented by dates, the problems associated with online dating, the problems associated with meeting new people, the fear of rejection, and many more. There are also many other things that tend to block us from dating successfully. Many people ignore these things. These things are essential if you want to make your date successful. In this section, let us have a look at the pitfalls associated with dating.

Negative Self-Talk

How you feel about yourself and your self-esteem is important if you ever want to succeed in your life. How you feel about yourself directly affects how you feel about yourself. If you treat yourself properly, everyone will treat you properly as well. Similarly, if you treat yourself badly, you will be treated badly by others as well. This is a vicious circle that is difficult to escape. If you feel that you are unattractive, it will be reflected on your face, and you will genuinely start looking unattractive. Remember, confidence is all about faking until you make it. You need to become your own cheerleader. You need to focus on things that you love about yourself and ignore other things.

Taking No Action

Another problem that is often associated with dating is becoming passive or not taking any action at all. This happens when you are already in a relationship but is also seen in people who are single. These people lament about their singlehood but don't do anything about it. They don't go out to meet people; they don't join any dating sites either. They just like to wallow in their own sadness. Most of these people tend to blame the world instead of taking responsibility for their own failure. It is necessary to be accountable for your own actions.

Limiting Beliefs about Dating, Relationships & the Opposite Sex

These people tend to have negative ideas about dating. If you regularly think about how much you despise men, how awful dating is, and how each relationship is bad, then you will never find a positive relationship for yourself. Your thoughts are reflected in your life. If you want positive things to happen in your life, you need to think positively as well. Thinking positive is necessary because it makes you feel optimistic.

Excuses

We love to procrastinate. People procrastinate a lot. They tend to procrastinate in a variety of ways. You will always find a reason to avoid the task. Excuses are aplenty with people who love to procrastinate or are in general lazy.

Past Baggage

Everyone has baggage that they carry with them all the time. The only difference between happy people and sad people is that happy people keep their baggage locked and shut away while unhappy people display it all the time and lament over it. It is better to live in the present and think of the future. It is recommended to avoid thinking of the past as much as possible.

Excessive Judgments & Expectations

Many people have a lot of expectations from their dates. When their date does not meet their expectations, these people become frustrated. They stop caring about the date. It should be remembered that no one is perfect. Everyone has their pros and cons. It is necessary to concentrate on the positive aspects of your date and ignore the tiny faults. Keep your mind open and wide.

Fear of Rejection

Nobody likes rejection, but it is a very common concept in a person's life. If you care a lot about rejection, you will never succeed in your life. Some people are so afraid of the fear that they stop dating completely. They start believing that they are unattractive, and they are unappealing. Rejection is normal and to be expected. Do not take rejections personally and instead focus on how to improve yourself.

Social Anxiety

Some people are often shy and nervous around new people. This is fine, and almost everyone faces it. Unless you feel incapacitated or start getting panic attacks, it is okay to feel nervous while meeting new people. Extreme social anxiety is real, but not a lot of people face it. If you suffer from it, it is recommended to contact a therapist as soon as possible.

If you do not have any social anxiety disorder and just have a serious case of nerves, don't worry. With practice, your nerves will go away. Don't let your feelings and emotions stop you from living your life. It is impossible to control how others feel about you or how they react, but you can surely control how you feel about yourself.

Busyness

People are often busy with their day-to-day jobs. Many people also have a lot of responsibilities, as well. But this does not mean that you should stop dating at all. Singles often feel more comfortable working instead of dating. But try to go out from time to time to keep your life from getting too monotonous and dull.

Fear of Intimacy & Vulnerability

Dating means getting to know someone and finding out things about them. It also means forming a connection with a person. To form a connection with someone, you need to show them your vulnerabilities. You need to allow people in your personal space. If you do not like people breaching your circle, or if you are an excessively private person, dating may seem quite a daunting task to you. But this does not mean that you should not try it. Take things slow and work on your dating life gradually.

Seven Flirting Mistakes Women Make

One of the best ways to start a conversation with a man and to let him know that you like him and are interested in him is by flirting with him. Flirting is useful in a variety of ways. It not only conveys your interest, but it also shows that you are confident, bold, and that you know what you want and desire. It allows the guy to see your mysterious, mischievous, and feminine side. But flirting can also backfire if not done correctly. There are many things that can go wrong while flirting. Here is a small list of things that you should avoid while flirting.

Playing Games

Playing hard to get is okay if you want to increase tension, but overdoing it is never good. Playing a lot of mind games with men will make them despise you. It only works if used in limited amounts. Men have self-respect, which often borders on ego, and they will not chase you if you play mind games all the time. If you are genuinely interested in a guy, do not feign indifference or disinterest for a long time.

Being Disrespectful

Humor and sarcasm are great ways to diffuse tension. They also act as great flirting tools. Humor can keep things relaxed. Sarcasm helps you display your feisty and sparky side to your dream guy. But both these, if used improperly, can come off as mean-spirited. Your sarcasm and humor should not offend anyone, especially the guy you are interested in. Never embarrass him in front of people. It is okay to tease him from time to time, but never overdo it, or he will avoid you.

Being Whiny

Asking for help and other similar tactics are great methods of flirting for women. Men love when women ask for help, as it makes them feel like heroes. Similarly, if the help is related to something physical, the man can put his strength and physical prowess on display. Men love to show off how strong they are. But never overdo this. If you constantly ask for help and whine about your "weakness," the guy will think you are a nuisance. Asking for help is fine; *being whiny and entitled is not.* While asking for advice or help, do not complain about your friends, family, job, or other people in your life. Keep everything simple and limited.

Being Too Clingy

Guys like to have their boundaries set. They like to be "lone wolves." They do not appreciate women who act too clingy or possessive. While some amount of possessiveness is cute, too much of it can ruin a relationship. A small gesture such as a gentle brush of fingers or arms is seductive, but clinging to his arm all the time, especially when he is trying to socialize is cringy. This is especially true if you have just met him. Do not act too clingy or envious. If you start getting too jealous, he will think that you are a neurotic person and will move away from you.

Coming On Too Strong

Along with clinginess, you need to avoid coming on too strong as well. It is necessary to be mindful of the things you say, but it is also important to know how to say them. If you come onto a guy too hard, he will believe that you are interested in a hook up only and do not want anything else. Similarly, making a lot of jokes about hooking up, or sexual jokes, will make him think that you are there for sex only. If you are looking for something serious, then it is recommended to take things slowly and let them develop gradually.

Time of Flirting

Everything has a proper time and place. Similarly, there are good times to flirt, and there are bad times to flirt as well. If a guy is looking excessively sad or extremely angry, it is recommended to steer clear of him. You should avoid flirting if he looks frustrated. Anger, frustration, and similar feelings distract people. The guy will not be able to concentrate on you or your advances. He may even react negatively to your flirting. In some cases, flirting will make him smile and therefore improve his mood. So, it depends on the circumstance and time whether to flirt or not.

Flirting in a Professional Setting

You should avoid flirting in a professional setting at all costs. This includes flirting in the office, at office parties, or professional meetings as well. If you flirt on such occasions, people may think that you are a sycophant; this may affect your career negatively.

Flirting Backfire

Flirting is a great way to introduce yourself to new people, but flirting can backfire sometimes. Everyone uses flirting to get things done with ease. For instance, a simple, flirtatious smile while bargaining, or a flirtatious banter with a barista, etc. Some women also use specific, and seductive lilt of their voice to ask for help.

People who are experts in the art of flirting know how to bat the eyelashes and cast suggestive looks to get things done for them. They can use these methods to find allies, friends, and social power. It is recommended to use each tool you have in your arsenal to get ahead of everyone. It is highly efficient to use your weapons when they are needed.

Erotic capital and prowess can really change the game for you. These are two gifts that can be used to get whatever you want, whether it is physical, material, or mental. Erotic capital is a combination of social as well as physical attractiveness. Flirting is one of the many techniques that are associated with this capital. Charisma and charm are a part of flirting that is appropriate and recommended for all kinds of situations.

While it is true that flirting can help you sometimes, it won't always help you. It can even backfire if you are not careful. For instance, flirting makes you vulnerable to judgment and misunderstandings. People can form misperceptions about you. It can even lead to a social backlash, as well. Experts believe that flirting is good for business, but it involves taking a lot of risks that can lead to various problems as well.

Flirting suggests the possibility of something sexual that may happen between individuals. It expressed with words, with the pauses, tone of voice, the posture of a person, eye contact, wordplay, gestures, and body language. Harmless flirting can help you a lot, but if the context of the flirting is not understood or if it is misread, then harmless flirting may evolve into something totally different. For instance, flirting in a bar is different than flirting for getting out of a speed ticket.

Many women tend to use flirting to get out of difficulties, such as a speeding ticket. While it is a tried and tested method to get away for free, some policemen may feel insulted by the obvious flirting and manipulation. Therefore, instead of getting away for free, you may land into even more trouble. It may even get you arrested.

The workplace often sets the scene for misunderstandings, as it is often easy to misconstrue intentions and ideas in the workplace. Many employees tend to employ flirting with improving their chances of getting a promotion or getting in the good graces of their employers. Similarly, many salespeople try to use the art of flirting and cajoling to attract customers. But if this kind of flirting is misread or misunderstood, your credibility may come under fire. People may even start to question your character and your intentions, as well. It will surely break down the trust between you, your employers, and your customers. In worse case scenarios, you may get fired, or a complaint may get registered against you. Therefore, many experts do not recommend workplace flirting. It is always better to keep things simple and professional at a professional place.

Some other experts believe that workplace flirting can work wonders. If the person who plans to flirt is an expert at flirting, he or she will not get into difficult situations. These experts believe that flirting only backfires for people who cannot flirt properly. Such people lack good judgment and do not possess the skills required to flirt efficiently. To flirt successfully without creating any problems, a person needs to understand the situation, time, place, and the person he or she is trying to flirt with. Only then can he or she flirt properly without any problem.

But then other professionals believe that sometimes even experts fail. While an expert flirter is well accustomed to his or her style and method of flirting, the opposite party may still feel objectified and insulted. This is a serious problem at workplaces because reputation and respect matter a lot in such big organizations.

Ultimately, flirting can make things extremely difficult for you if you do not know how and when and where to do it. Flirting blurs the line between your intentions and what you say. This may confuse a lot of people, which may lead to misunderstanding. Misunderstandings can lead to grave results in professional settings. Therefore, it is recommended to avoid flirting in the workplace and reserve it for bars and clubs only.

Chapter Fourteen: But, Is He Mr. Right?

If you have been dating a man for a long time, this question is bound to come into your mind soon. This question has plagued a lot of women since the beginning of time. It is a serious question that has only two options. This infamous question is, "Is he serious about me?"

Women are constantly plagued by this question due to the lack of connection between men and women. Men do not understand the feelings of women, while women don't understand what men want. Women get confused about what men want because often men do not know what they want for themselves, and this confusion is reflected onto women. Due to this confusion, women tend to overthink and scrutinize even the smallest details. This hair-splitting activity leads to a lot of stress and undue pressure. When this happens, women tend to lose all their hope about a new, budding relationship. They start thinking that they will never get a man to stay. They also become suspicious of men's intentions and judge them all the time. This is why it is better to form a connection with your boyfriend as soon as possible.

Many times, it so happens that when you start relaxing and enjoying the bliss of a long-term relationship, the guy you are in love with starts to become distant. He starts to move away gradually from you. When this happens, women start to relive every living moment of their existence just to check what they did wrong. They tend to recheck every sentence, every word, every action, and every object that they ever said or experienced with their man. This is done to find the root cause of the problem - but usually, all this exercise is in vain.

If a man is serious about you, he will display it through his actions. But rest assured, if he does not show this, it is not because you did something wrong. If a guy does not want to commit, it is his problem. There is nothing wrong with you. Men tend to be indecisive about a lot of things. Many times, they do not know or understand what they really desire due to a multitude of options. But instead of being suspicious of them, it is recommended to give them their time and space to come up with a decision on their own. If you feel that they are taking too long, wait some more. If still, he does not want to commit, maybe it is time for you to have a serious, life-changing talk.

When men are serious about you, they will flaunt it with pride. They will let you know that they are genuinely serious about you through their actions, gestures, words, expressions, etc. You can observe whether a man is serious about you or not by observing his or her behavior. By observing these signs in his behavior, you can save yourself from unnecessary trouble, pain, and overthinking. You just need to pay attention to his behavior. Here is a small list of 20 things that men tend to do when they are serious about you. If your man displays most of these signs, then congratulations, you are in for the long game.

Priority

Men have a lot of things going on in their lives. This is especially true if the man is a career-oriented person. Still, if you are his number one priority, then rest assured, he is serious about you. What does being someone's number one priority mean? It means that the man will always have time for you, even when he is busy. He will refrain from making excuses about not talking to you or meeting you. He will tend to go out of his way just to meet you. If he is really interested in you, he will try to make things happen in such a way that he and you will be together all the time. He will not lie or use excuses while talking to you.

Deeper Level

As said above, many women are plagued with the question, "Is he serious about me?" This question has ruined a lot of lives. It is a classic problem that seemingly has no solution. But there are certain things that can help you to solve this question. Whenever you think "Is he serious about me?" start thinking instead about, "Is he *curious* about me?"

If a man is curious about you, then he is invested and interested in the things that are going on in your day-to-day life. He wants to know your likes, your dislikes, your fears, your passions, things that make you nervous, things that you prefer, your favorite food, your favorite book, your favorite TV show, etc. He does not want to know these things just for the sake of it; he wants to know them because he is genuinely interested in you and wants to get to know you better. He wants to understand you on a deeper level and is therefore serious about you.

He Listens to You and Asks for Your Opinion

Men are lone wolves; they rarely take advice and suggestions. Therefore, the classic "not asking for directions" stereotype has been perpetuated so much. Men are often bad listeners, as well. So, if you see your man listening to each word carefully and hanging onto them, then you can be sure that he likes you and is serious about you.

To make the deal sweeter, if he asks you your opinion about things, especially in his personal life, then it means that you mean something to him. He appreciates your ideas and thoughts. He wants to understand your perspective on some levels because he respects you and loves you.

Listening is one of the easiest ways to check whether a person is interested in someone or not. You can never force a person to pay attention to something, especially if they are not interested in it. This is why if a man is paying attention to you and is waiting for your advice, then he is a keeper. He is surely serious about you.

He Trusts You

Trust is a crucial aspect and the basis of relationships and dating. Without trust, no date or relationship can survive. Without trust, it is impossible to form the foundation of a healthy relationship. But testing whether a man trusts you or not can be slightly complex. If done incorrectly, for instance, pranking him with a "cheating" prank can break his trust forever. Instead, there are many simple, obvious, but often ignored ways that can be used to check whether a guy trusts you or not.

If a guy trusts you, he will be honest and open with you. He will feel comfortable talking about his fears, feelings, emotions, and similar things with you. He will be honest with you and will let you know things about his life. If he can be honest with you, then he trusts you with his soul. If you are the first person with whom he shares his life-events, then he surely loves you and is serious about you. He wants to share things first with you because he wants you to understand how special you are.

You're Spending More and More Time Together

In the initial stages of a relationship, couples tend to spend a couple of hours with each other every other day. The time you spend with your partner is based on a lot of things, but on average, in the initial stages, the number of meetings is few, and the duration of meetings is less.

In the initial stages of a relationship, couples tend to meet for just a couple of dates per week. But with time, the intensity of the relationship increases, and the couple starts to meet more and more. They start to spend more time together. This is also an indicator of the man being seriously into you. If he were not into you, he would have escaped long ago. If he initiates the dates himself, then rest assured he is crazy for you.

If the guy is not interested in you, he will make many excuses to avoid spending time with you. But if he goes out of his way and cancels stuff just because he wants to be with you, then rest assured he is really into you and would like to take things further. This man is a keeper, and you should not let him go.

He Pays Attention to Little Details

Women are extremely meticulous. We have a fine eye for detail. We pay close attention to things that often go unnoticed by men. Therefore, they cannot tell the difference between mauve and lavender. This does not mean that men are born without the ability to perceive details. They do, but it is just that they do not find them interesting enough to retain. A man's mind does not care about minutiae; he only pays attention to details when he is seriously invested in something or someone. Therefore, if your man remembers all the important dates, your favorite things, your complex coffee order, or notices things like a simple haircut, then he is serious about you. He notices these things because he is observing you. And along with the observation, he is also paying attention to minute details, the things that are happening in your life, and what is important to you.

He Keeps His Promises

Men have traditionally been associated with the role of heart breakers. These "bad boys" do not care about anything and are notorious for breaking their promises. While these are some unfortunate stereotypes, men do not consider promises to be important. Women are more likely to keep promises as compared to men. But as said above, relationships are built on trust and mutual respect. If your beau keeps his promises all the time, then he surely cares about you.

If he promised you to take you to dinner at the end of the week and follow it through, then you are in luck. Many men who are not serious tend to break their promises by making random excuses. They try to get out of their promises. Nothing is sexier than a man who can keep his word and can stick to his promises. Such men never disappoint anyone because they know that promises have feelings and emotions as a base. Even if he screws up (after all he is a human being), he will apologize profusely and will try to make it up to you.

He Shows His Love with Actions

If a man is serious about you, he will not only say it. He will always try to prove it to you through his actions, as well as his gestures and body language. He will appreciate you and will shower his affection on you as well. He will also comfort you whenever you feel sad or depressed. He will try to surprise you and will make you coffee in the morning. He will do anything just to see you smile. He understands that his proclamations of love are useless if he cannot follow them through and act upon them. This is why he will always be ready to try and prove his love for you as well.

He's Excited About You When You Aren't Around

A guy who is serious about you tends to talk about you all the time, even in your absence. If your friends and family complain to you all the time just because your boyfriend talks about you all the time, then he is surely in love with you. A man talks about a woman all the time because he is genuinely interested in her, and she is on his mind all the time. Many times, men fall in love with a woman's absence. If he goes crazy whenever you are not with him, it means that he has fallen for you and is in love with you.

He Makes Plans with You in Advance and Sticks to Them

If a man is serious about you, he will make plans in advance and will always try to think of new ideas to have fun with you. He never worries you about things. He is never absent. He will always have something planned for your entertainment. He makes your life exciting and worth living. No matter how busy he is, he will try to find time for you. He will make plans with you and will keep the plans as well.

He Always Looks for Ways to Include You in His Interests

He shares your passion with you. He also shares your hobbies with you. He looks out for you. If both of you are interested in two distinct things, he tries to incorporate you into his activities, and he tries to participate in yours as well. He does not keep things to himself because he likes to share things with you. He wants to be an integral part of your life and vice versa as well. He tries hard to understand your passions, your interests, and your hobbies as well.

You've Met His Friends and Family

If a guy is serious about you, he will want you to meet his parents, family, and friends. In fact, if a guy wants you to meet his parents, then it is the ultimate sign that he is really interested in you and wants to take things further.

If a guy takes you for granted or tries to gaslight you, then he will never want you to meet his parents. He will refrain from meeting his family and friends as well because he has no intention of staying with you.

If he does let you meet his parents, then he is genuinely in love with you. It also means that he is proud of you and wants to share your presence with everyone. He wants people to know that he loves you and appreciates you. He wants everyone to know that you are the one who is meant for him.

He Treats You Like a Lady

A man who is genuinely in love with you will always treat you like a lady. He will not make you wait, and if he does, he will apologize profusely. He will always treat you with respect. He will always open doors for you. If he ever commits a mistake, he will ask for your forgiveness. He will never rush you into things. He will appreciate your decisions. He will never force you to do anything that you are not comfortable with. Your happiness and respect are his number one priority. He treats you like a lady because he knows that you are a lady. He wants you to feel like a lady, as well. He wants you to feel proud of him. He wants you to feel safe with him.

He is Punctual

A guy who is genuinely interested in you will try to be punctual. He will try to be on time for dates. If he ever arrives late, he will apologize. This shows his respect and cares for you. If a man does not care for you, he won't even try to be on time. He will never apologize if he ever arrives late. If a man is not serious about someone, he does not care for them. He does not feel that he should apologize to a person about whom he does not care because there is no sense of attachment present between you and him. Men possess empathy, but it is often selective.

He Regularly Initiates Contact with You

He calls you first, sends you random texts, and promises you that he will call later when he misses your call. You do not need to worry about his manipulative behavior because he never manipulates you. Similarly, he does not lie to you either. He does not make any excuses if he messes up. Rather, he apologizes in an honest manner. He initiates contact with you, and you rarely must wonder where he is. He likes to tell you about his plans for the day. He informs you well in advance if he isn't available for a long period of time.

You Have Fun Together

If his eyes lit up when you are with him, and he genuinely laughs at your jokes, then he is really interested in you. He genuinely cares about you and appreciates you a lot. He does not act reserved around you, and similarly, he does not play hard to get. You should not play hard to get, either. You feel relaxed with him, and whenever you are going to be absent from each other, he always appreciates you for spending time with you.

When a man is serious about you, he looks at things from a different point of view. He wants to enjoy the relationship and have a lot of fun with you. He wants to be your partner in crime. He enjoys things and likes spending time with you. He is not just interested in having sex with you, but he is more interested in being with you. This is the main difference between men who are genuinely in love with you and those who are faking it just to get into your pants.

He Talks About Future Plans

Everyone likes to talk about their future, but if a man talks to you about his future with you, then he is serious about you. He is genuinely interested in you and wants to spend the rest of his life with you. He does not take you for granted. Every second that he spends with you matters a lot to him. He is happy to spend time with you and envisions a future with you. He wants to go on long journeys with you. He is not just focused on the present, but he wants to spend time and discuss the future of your relationship as well.

He Shares Everything with You

A guy who is serious about you will share his dreams, his thoughts, his ideas, and his fears with you as well. If something angers him, he does not try to confront you. Instead, he thinks about the incident calmly and talks to you about it. He considers your opinion on the matter to be crucial. He encourages you to be open to him as well. This is how the relationship thrives and survives properly.

He Tries to Resolve Arguments

No relationship is perfect, and each couple goes through ups and downs all the time. In fact, many people say that if a couple does not fight with each other, they are not true love. Couples are bound to fall into arguments frequently.

Now that it is settled that every couple fight, why should you care? The main factor in this argument is not that all couples fight, but rather *in the way this fight is resolved*. All couples fight, but the difference between successful couples and regular (or failed) couples is that successful couples solve their problems properly. The guy who cares about you will deal with the arguments properly. A guy who is serious about you will try to solve the problems without letting them escalate. The guy who loves you will not make you feel bad or sad about the argument. He will not insult you just because he is mad at you.

A guy who is serious about you rarely loses his temper with you. Even if he loses his temper, he will never insult you. He will pick his words properly because he knows that he does not want to lose you ever.

He's Open about Your Relationship

Whenever you meet his friends or colleagues, he introduces you as soon as possible. He never misses any chance to introduce you to his friends or family. He is proud of you and is open about your relationship as well. He wants the whole world to know that you are dating each other. He always holds your hand when you walk together.

If other girls ever show interest in him, he declines them politely by letting them know about your existence. He tells everyone that he is taken immediately.

Therefore, if your boyfriend shows some or all the above signs, then rest assured, he is serious about you. Now you do not need to worry about whether your boyfriend loves you or not. He is a keeper and wants to be with you forever.

Chapter Fifteen: 25 Seductive Hacks to Keep Things Juicy Long Term

The media all around us always talk about how women can have better orgasms, better sex, or a better relationship. These sources also come up with various tips to do so. But these tips rarely work because they do not understand the intricate nuances of the female psyche and thinking.

Many times, we love our boyfriend or partner. But love does not equal a healthy sex life. Quite often, sex may turn into a regular ordeal if you do not know how to spice it up. There is nothing worse than sex becoming boring. Keeping your sex life active and healthy is essential for any relationship to survive. Not many people know that this is a common problem. Sex tends to become predictable and routine, often in a long-term relationship. The intensity and the chemistry that is present in the initial stages of a relationship fades away with time. While it is true that it is impossible to go back into time to relive those moments, it does not mean that you cannot bring back the passion once again. In this section, let us have a look at how you can spice up your sex life to avoid it from becoming routine and boring.

Initiation

Long-term relationships bring with them a lot of things, such as comfort, relaxation, love, and calmness. But they also make partners take each other for granted. Partners stop making any effort to feel more attractive and keep the relationship exciting because they already know that the relationship is not going anywhere. This pattern also gets repeated in your sex life.

Women are often stereotyped as coy and coquettish. They are not expected to initiate sex often. But this is an old stereotype. If you want to keep your relationship and sex life active and exciting, you need to break the boundaries and destroy the stereotypes.

Initiating sex should not seem like a task. For instance, many people initiate sex at the end of the day when both the partners are already exhausted and just want to sleep. Therefore, sex becomes a task or a "before bed" activity. To spice things up, initiate sex at random moments, especially when your partner does not expect it at all. For instance, initiate it in the morning right after he gets out of the shower or while he is tossing a salad. This will surely spice up your sex life.

Be a Tease

Being a tease and acting playful can really make your sex life pop. Being a tease does not require a lot of time or preparation. Simple dirty talking is one of the best ways to be a tease. Men love dirty talk. Try dirty talking at inappropriate places where sex is impossible, for instance, while dining out or while in a theatre. This will keep things exciting and will drive him crazy.

You can also do this during sex itself. Quite often, sex becomes a routine task for long-term partners, which is why they end up hurrying. They just want to get it over with. Instead of doing this, you can prolong the sexual activity by teasing him as long as he can stand it. Get him on the brink of orgasm and then hold back. Wait, and continue. This will drive him crazy and will make things absolutely sexy for both of you.

Surprises

One of the best things to keep a relationship exciting and fun is the element of surprise. To keep the fire burning, try to surprise your partner from time to time. Get back home before your boyfriend sometimes, and as soon as he comes back, take him straight to the bedroom. You can also welcome him wearing nothing but your birthday suit. Beware and ensure that he is alone before you do this.

Plan a Romantic Weekend Getaway

Surprise your boyfriend with an impromptu trip just for the two of you. Vacations are expensive, and often time-consuming, but it is not difficult to do one on a limited budget. It is fine if you can afford just a night away. Even a single night vacation can work wonders for your relationship. Your partner will surely appreciate the effort and thought that you put into the trip. He will also enjoy the change of scenery. And there is surely nothing better than spending some quality time with your loved one.

Wear Lingerie

Lingerie can really spice up things for you, especially in a long-term relationship. When we are in a long-term relationship, we tend to let go of ourselves. Both the partners start wearing random clothes, sweatshirts, ratty tees, etc. While this is a great thing as it allows you to be cozy and comfortable with each other, it kills the sexual intensity and attraction. Lingerie can help you light the fire once again. You can surprise your partner with a new set of lingerie or ask him for help while buying one. Enter the bed while wearing a sexy, hot negligee and invite him to your bed. Or, slip into something seductive while he is watching TV and crawl into his arms. Lingerie can make things spicy for both partners.

Pretend to be Strangers

This is another way to spice up things. It has been shown in many popular shows as well. If you have a good sense of humor and both of you can act (no need to follow Stanislavski), you can act like strangers meeting for the first time. Meet at random places or meet where you had your first date. In this method, you need to pretend that you have just met for the very first time. Seduce each other and hit on each other.

Take Charge for the Night

Another thing to make things sexy is by taking charge of the night. By taking charge of things, this means taking control of everything. Make all the decisions and lead him into them. If your boyfriend does not like being passive in general, he will surely enjoy this change. It will allow him to relax and take things slowly. Have your way with him and take your sex and relationship to the next level.

Let Him Be in Charge

You can make things spicy by doing the exact opposite of the last tip. Let your boyfriend take charge of the night. To make things kinkier, tell him that you will be his servant tonight and will allow him to do whatever he wants (do keep in mind that both of you still need to respect each other's boundaries."

Props

You can use many kinds of props to spice up your seduction game. For instance, wearing lacy lingerie and teasing him using the laces can bring on the game. Similarly, you can use melted chocolates, strawberries, etc. to heat things up. Eating strawberries slowly and seductively while holding eye contact is incredibly sexy and erotic. You can also eat melted chocolates. Don't be scared to get dirty.

No Hands Rule

You can make the foreplay interesting by bringing in the no-hands rule. For this rule, the man can do things, but he cannot use his hands. Tease him throughout this game and watch him moan with pleasure. Your man will come up with many different creative ways to follow this rule.

Text Dirty

Texting is a great way to seduce your man, especially at inappropriate times. For instance, if he is at work, send him a sexy text and tell him what you plan to do with him that night. This will keep him on his toes throughout the day, and the anticipation will make things spicy at night.

Send Pictures

Nudes can be classy too! Instead of sending him random pictures of your genitals or breasts, make them erotic and seductive. For instance, a transparent top or a short skirt that barely covers your buttocks will make you look sexier than being in your birthday suit. Click some pictures wearing these clothes, in suggestive posts and forward them to him. He will be flabbergasted and will rush home soon. Beware of sending these photos to casual lovers because you never know when they may just turn up on the Internet to haunt you.

Take Him Shopping

Shopping can be quite a boring task for many men, but this does not mean that you cannot use it for the purpose of seduction. Ask him to accompany you shopping. He will act grumpy and mean, but gradually take him into a lingerie shop. You will see his frown changed into a large smile, and his eyes light up. Offer him some sneak peeks from the trial room. Whisper in his ears about the lingerie.

Seductive Looks

In a long-term relationship, sex often gets boring. Partners stop caring how they look. Quite often, people wear pajamas, buns, and sweatshirts. But breaking the monotony can help you spice things up. For instance, occasionally, dress up for him in your best clothes. Look sexy with slight makeup, sexy hair, and clothes that leave nothing to the imagination.

Undress

Once you show him your clothes, now it is time to show him what is underneath. Clothes are like wrapping paper, while your body is his gift. Act clueless and seductively while slowly removing your clothes. Stripping casually but seductively is one of the best ways to seduce a man.

Foreplay and Tease

Intense foreplay can help you keep things heated. Give him everything and lead him on, only to break the play before the final act. Tell him that you are going for a shower, or just excuse yourself by saying that you have work. This will enhance his cravings for you. He will feel frustrated and will moan with passion.

Shower Together

Sneak casually into the bathroom when he is showering. Do this when he expects it the least. Showering together is incredibly sexy. A sexy shower will make your mornings brighter and bolder.

Leave your Fragrance

If you have a favorite fragrance, use it as an asset. Spray it around in certain places that will remind him of you. Your aroma will surely tantalize him. Don't overdo this, though, as some people may find it irritating.

Create the Mood

Creating the mood for sex is not difficult. Playing seductive and romantic music, lighting scented candles, wearing a negligee, decorating your room with flowers such as red roses, etc. are easy ways to set the mood of the room. You can also personalize the room by adding things that are special to you. For instance, certain items may trigger memories of good and sexy times.

Be His Masseuse

Massages are incredibly relaxing, but they are also incredibly sexy. Give him massages frequently and touch his erogenous zones. For instance, bite his earlobes, kiss his throat, touch his navel, etc. Touching erogenous zones can make a man go mad with pleasure.

Plan a Romantic Weekend

This is another extension of the vacation plan. If you cannot plan a vacation, plan a romantic getaway. Surprise him with a simple stay at a luxurious hotel. This will not only enhance your sexual relationship, but it will also make your emotional bond stronger. Making emotional bonds strong is as necessary as a strong sexual relationship.

Play Strip Poker

Another thing that can make your sex life more interesting is by playing strip poker. There are various versions of strip poker available online. You can also personalize strip poker according to your needs. Let your creative juices flow.

Roleplay

Roleplay is a great way to heat things up in the bedroom. Share your fantasies with him and ask him to share his with you. Also, ask him which characters he loves, and which stars he finds the hottest. Then, one day, surprise him by roleplaying his dream character. Use your acting and makeup skills to attract him and make the illusion stronger.

Touch Him in Public

Touching in public is a great way to make him go crazy with passion. For instance, when you are eating out, move your naked feet over so they touch his leg. Or gently touch him under the table and then touch yourself. Winking, raw kisses, etc., will drive him crazy as well. Don't go overboard and keep things under the PG level while in public.

Try a New Position in Bed

Try out some new positions in bed. You do not need to choose the difficult ones that require the precision and flexibility of a yogi or a contortion artist. Just be yourself and guide him through this new experience. There are many easy positions available online, so check them out.

Learn a Few Erotic Moves

Dancing is incredibly sexy unless you are born with two left feet. Making the right dance moves will make him go crazy. To make things sexier, wear sexy attire, and learn some seductive moves online. You can also add some stripping to make things sexier. Remember, seduction is about hiding things and revealing them one by one.

Therefore, these are 25 tried and tested ways that can help you charm and seduce your man. The art of seduction is not complicated, but it requires some practice. You need to be charming and playful. A lot of charm and a lot of eroticisms will make your man go crazy with pleasure. Remember, it is more about hiding and not about revealing. You should always leave him wanting more.

Plan your game properly and follow it carefully, but don't be afraid of changing things or breaking the rules if it means infinite pleasure. A little creativity and a little boldness will make your bedroom a room of pleasure.

Conclusion

Flirting is a bold and huge topic. It entails a lot of things that cannot be covered in such a small book. There are many different facets associated with flirting that makes flirting so complex. Flirting is a highly cultural thing. It changes from culture to culture. In fact, it can change according to the region as well.

This book can really work wonders in the lives of single women. If you do not feel confident about flirting with a man, the methods and techniques mentioned in the book will help you to attract your crush.

The chapters given in this book have been tried and tested. They are bound to work. The instructions given in this book are easy to follow. Anyone can follow them.

Confidence is essential for any job. If you are not confident, you won't be able to flirt with the man of your dreams successfully. Therefore, a detailed chapter on confidence-building has been covered in this book.

Flirting works on multiple levels, out of which physical and verbal are the two most important levels. Both levels have been covered extensively in this book. A detailed chapter on body language will help you achieve your goals with ease.

Remember that flirting is supposed to be an organic thing. There is no blueprint for successful flirting; still, the tips provided in this book should be used as stepping-stones.

Due to these and many other qualities, this book is surely one of the best books about flirting available on the market. Women who use the methods given in this book are sure to find a high-value man and will spend the rest of their life with him knowing *how to keep him interested.*

Reference

https://www.mookychick.co.uk/how-to/how-to-guides/how-to-seduce-like-cleopatra.php

https://www.cosmopolitan.com/sex-love/a23583489/passionate-kisses/

Vea más libros escritos por Dara Montano

SELF-ESTEEM FOR
Women

THE ULTIMATE SELF-HELP GUIDE TO
BUILDING HABITS THAT WILL IMPROVE YOUR CONFIDENCE,
SELF-COMPASSION, ASSERTIVENESS, SELF-LOVE,
AND MINDSET

DARA MONTANO

www.ingramcontent.com/pod-product-compliance
Lightning Source LLC
Chambersburg PA
CBHW070759300326
41914CB00053B/741